"Cindy is a brilliant and gifted healer, combining her depth of neuroscientific knowledge with potent intuition. Her book, *Soul Bridges*, is a critical tool for identifying the blocks in our lives that hold us back and transforming them into higher self-teachings. The *Soulercise* techniques in this book are immediately accessible to anyone looking for spiritual and personal development. They have helped me grow as both a human being and a leader."
—Anderson Pugash, Sound Healer & Hospitality Entrepreneur

"*Soulercise* is a foundational practice for anyone interested in experiencing freedom from stress and fear-based patterning. This unique program is the most compassionate and practical I have come across in my 20 years of personal development work. Thank you, Cindy, for creating this bridge to the Soul for us all."
—Heather H.

"*Soulercise* is a powerful process that I have benefited from in so many ways. Most significantly, after using this advanced tool, I am finally free from painful emotions that were stuck deep within me. I can now clear them up on my own."
—Laura M.

SOUL BRIDGES

SOUL BRIDGES

A PATHWAY TO SELF-DISCOVERY AND ENLIGHTENMENT

CINDY REYNOLDS

ENDLESS PULSE, LLC

2nd Edition
© Copyright 1998–2023, Endless Pulse, LLC

All rights reserved. No part of this manuscript may be reproduced (by any means) or utilized in any form, electronic or mechanical, without the written permission of Cindy Reynolds or Endless Pulse, LLC.

ISBN (paperback): 978-1-7375237-2-7
ISBN (ebook): 978-1-7375237-3-4

Editing: Doug Childers; Valerie Costa
Cover Design: *the*BookDesigners
Cover Image: Shutterstock.com
Interior design: Christy Day, Constellation Book Services
Author Photo: Steven Underwood

Printed in the United States of America

Soulercise® & NeuroFit® are Registered Trademarks of Cindy Reynolds

This book is lovingly dedicated to the Beings of Light who guide and protect us on our path through life.
 — Thank you!

Contents

Introduction — 1

Chapter 1: Soul Food — 9
Chapter 2: Soul & Personality — 17
Chapter 3: Thoughts are Things — 29
Chapter 4: States of Emotion — 40
Chapter 5: How to Soulercise — 51
Chapter 6: Difficult Situations — 64
Chapter 7: Personality Thoughts & Emotions — 76
Chapter 8: The Turning Point — 90
Chapter 9: Soul Thoughts & Emotions — 101
Chapter 10: Soul Fitness — 115
Chapter 11: Master Daily Life — 127
Chapter 12: The Brain Connection — 140

Acknowledgements — 161

Introduction

Have you ever felt as if you are on a roller coaster riding up and down through all of the success and failure, heartache, and joy of life on Earth? What if you could relax on the ride and respond to and appreciate each event, even the most difficult, from a place of mastery, wisdom, and strength?

What if you could hear a wise inner voice offering enlightened guidance, revealing the deeper meanings behind life's chaos and disappointments? And, what if you could maintain the peace of meditation amidst life's everyday frustrations and grow through all of your experiences?

Yearnings like these first emerged within me at the age of twelve, when the sudden death of my beloved grandmother and the life-threatening disease of my younger sister left me shaken to the core. In the aftermath of shock, confusion, and trauma, I began to pray for help and long for freedom from my fears.

The series of tragic events that followed over years—the prolonged illness of my sister, the sudden death of my husband, and the concussions, devastating illnesses, and eventual passing of my only daughter—intensified my search for meaning and my yearning for insight. It is no surprise, and perhaps no accident, that I became a seeker, and meditation became a way of life.

Through these unrelenting traumas, phenomena beyond the range of my five senses spurred me on, guiding me in my search to discover the truth of who I am in spirit. One of the most dramatic instances occurred the night my husband, Peter, passed on. Overcome once again by the trauma of sudden death, I lay alone weeping and praying in the dark. I cried out for help from the depths of my being.

Within moments, a whirling ball of light encircled the room. I heard a loud buzzing in my ears as an electrical current coursed through me. Drawn out of my body, I floated effortlessly for several moments above the shell of the "physical me" lying motionless on the bed.

Then I was rocketed out of the room into another dimension. My Soul body soared through darkness and light in the serene vastness of the universe.

Suddenly, a Romanesque temple with long white stairs and tall marble pillars appeared before me, as real as the room I'd just left. Pete, who had just passed on, was standing on the stairs! We were instantly transported to a large hall where a group of sage-like beings in white robes sat illumined around a long mahogany-like table. They took turns communicating, telepathically and lovingly. They said:

"Where we are now, this is home. The Earth plane is your training ground, your temporary school of life. No matter how hard your lessons or how difficult life becomes, you have chosen to go there to learn from your experiences."

"Together with us you choose your family, your time and place of birth, and the specific situations that will challenge you and give your Soul the best opportunity to evolve. This is your true higher purpose for entering the Earth plane."

Introduction

"In one mortal lifetime, you will attempt to master at the most two or three challenging emotions. Observe yourself in daily life. Get to know who you are. And in the face of difficulties, choose who you want to be."

"Take time each day to go within, charge your system and cultivate the power of Soul consciousness."

We were then taken to another section of the temple where a movie screen appeared before me, showing scenes from my life and how I had handled them. During my "life review," there was no judgement only love and support. And more messages were given from the Beings of Light: "You are to act as a bridge between the seen and unseen—between the physical body and the eternal Soul. And through the written word, you will provide the steps necessary to master the higher purpose of life on Earth."

I visited with Pete for a bit longer, and then as quickly as I had left my body I returned to it, overwhelmed by the profundity of the experience. Feelings of awe mingled with my grief over the loss of Peter. I had so many questions.

"What does it mean to master my emotions and choose who I want to be?"

"How am I supposed to 'charge my system' and 'cultivate the power' of Soul consciousness?"

"Do we review our life as if from a movie screen in dimensions unseen?"

I felt certain that the answers would be revealed to me over time. But several things were clear: Intelligent beings exist beyond this Earth plane—defined in the Oxford Dictionary as "the realm of the living, as opposed to that of the spirits."

I am not only a physical self; I am also a being of light, an eternal Soul. And this essential part of me that survives the death of my physical body is a powerful and intelligent guiding force existing within me right now.

In the light of that experience, I made a vow to apply these teachings to every part of my life and to find a way to share with others all I had been given. But it would take me years to fully comprehend and integrate this profound experience.

As time passed, my grief over Peter's death gradually diminished. I began to recognize my life as a spiritual process, and I continued to ask for guidance along the way. Books, teachers, and new meditation techniques materialized when needed and provided answers to the profound questions circling within me.

As I continued to observe myself daily, I discerned recurring patterns in the difficult emotions that cycled through me. And deeper meanings hidden behind life's seeming chaos gradually emerged. The more I coached myself to choose who I wanted to be in the face of life's challenges, the more I practiced living in new ways.

Eventually, I began to understand my out-of-body experience (OBE) and the declarations of the Beings of Light. I learned to "run energy" and charge my system with the power required to maintain my Soul's perspective. And I started a practice of life review when confronted with difficult situations. Insights that arose from reflection and experience became transformative steps to fulfilling my higher purpose.

I know I'm not alone on this journey. You, too, may have yearned for freedom from life's pain, disappointments, and traumas. You, too, may have wondered: "Who am I?"

"Why am I here?"

"What is my higher purpose?"

"What is the bigger picture, the unseen reality behind the seeming chaos of my life?"

Introduction

"Do beings of light truly watch over us?"

"Do miracles really happen?"

And finally, "What will become of 'me' when this physical body dies?"

You may have begun to search for answers to these profound questions, hoping to draw the light of eternity into your human existence. You may be engaging in spiritual study, meditation, prayer, service, and more. And in quiet moments, you may have experienced the light, intelligence, and power of your Soul and its eternal source.

But how do we persevere in our positive intentions when we are confronted again and again with adversity in our lives? How do we maintain this Soul consciousness and manifest our higher purpose when outer events and negative or critical inner voices, programmed into us since birth, create sadness, fear, insecurity, shame, and despair?

The *Soulercise®* process explained in this book offers a way. Through this unique Soul fitness program, you are given 7 Steps to evolve into higher states of enlightenment while facing adversity, eventually fulfilling your higher purpose for being on Earth.

As you go through this process of self-discovery, you'll learn to recognize and release negative thoughts and beliefs that operate in us like unconscious disempowering programs. You'll learn to replace these recurring conditioned inner broadcasts with higher, empowering Soul perspectives and healthy emotional responses to difficult circumstances. You'll begin to move confidently forward on the path of your Soul plan while identifying your specific challenging emotions and conducting life reviews while in your physical body.

We've incarnated in this material world in bodies made of indestructible subatomic particles and light-energy. And our Souls have come here to learn the lessons of life, to acquire knowledge and wisdom, and to help move forward the evolution of human consciousness into the realm of Soul consciousness.

Life will always throw us challenging curve balls. But as we learn to *Soulercise* and build bridges between our physical self—our personality and our higher self—our Soul, we can use the various moments and events of life as opportunities to practice living in a more enlightened way. We can meet life's challenges from a higher Soul perspective and learn to master our emotions.

As old negative or disempowering thoughts and beliefs begin to atrophy and fall away, we evolve and become clearer, lighter, stronger, and wiser. We gain a harvest of knowledge and wisdom that benefits us and influences and inspires others. Practicing these life skills over time deepens self-awareness and emotional mastery and etches new neuropathways in our brains.

Soulercise is my personal offering—the fruit of my life's purpose. It is a key component of the NeuroFit® "Cross-Train Your Brain" NeuroFitness program I developed in Marin County, CA, and a means by which I, too, can "walk the walk." Without the difficult road mapped out for me in this lifetime, I wouldn't be sharing or using this training today. And the same Soul power and force that catalyzed my out-of-body experience and that has so profoundly guided and transformed my life lies within each of us.

We are all beautiful and extraordinary multi-dimensional light beings, eternal Souls. As Soul consciousness becomes a living, breathing part of your daily life, may you, too, discover your higher purpose for being on Earth and walk into eternity with increasing mastery, love, and light.

Enjoy!!!

"To know thyself is the beginning of wisdom."

—Socrates

CHAPTER 1
Soul Food

*"The season of failure is the best time
for sowing the seeds of success."*

—Paramahansa Yogananda

Have you ever experienced the death or loss of a loved one; had a serious accident or illness; been deeply hurt or betrayed? Have you ever invested years of your life in a job believing you had established a secure future for yourself and perhaps your family, only to be suddenly laid off? What do you do when life delivers such devastating blows? How do you cope?

Will the difficulties in your journey through life crush and defeat you? Or will they become challenges that stretch you and Soul food that nourishes your growth on your path to self-discovery and enlightenment? Will you see life through the eyes of fear and grow small and cautious? Or will you see life through the eyes of your Soul and recognize everyone you meet and every situation you encounter as a potential steppingstone toward your greater good?

Believe it or not, you can choose how you respond, mentally and emotionally, to crises and challenges. You can choose to develop strength of character and effect changes in the world around you by your own determined acts of will. You can choose how you interpret what happens to you. And your choices can multiply your options, develop your character, and significantly impact your ability to fulfill your higher purpose.

LIFE'S CHALLENGING MOMENTS
In 2000, life served me another challenging dish of Soul food to digest. For several years I had been working long hours for a software company with a unique product. As the director of quality assurance, I had set up a Software Engineering - QA department and built a finely tuned, highly productive team. Then the market began to fall, angel investors got worried, funding began to dry up, and I received confidential news of inevitable company-wide layoffs.

On the morning of October 17th, an urgent email came across our company's computer screens: "Mandatory Company Conference Call! 11:00 a.m. sharp. All employees must attend!"

It was an unusual format for a company meeting. Sensing bad news, everyone was worried. But there was nothing I could say or do to help. I'd been informed of the layoffs to come and was sworn to secrecy. I knew that most of my team had been spared; only three out of eleven would be let go.

So, I sat silently at my desk, waiting. At 11:00 a.m., I dialed the number and the CEO came on the line. After a brief introduction he described the company's desperate situation and concluded with the dreaded phrase, "We have no choice but to let people go."

His diplomatic tone didn't soften the blow. He told everyone to sit by the phone for the next ten minutes and their manager would notify them if they were on the layoff list.

Immediately afterward, people congregated uneasily in the game room with their cell phones, waiting for a call. Managers and directors who hadn't been notified about the layoffs also waited for their phones to ring. I had the grim task of making three of those dreaded calls. That ten minutes, and those three calls to my now former team members, were excruciatingly painful!

I still had an eight-member QA team. Our department was still intact. But I was on guard. One round of layoffs might well become two. I didn't panic, but I was vigilant, watching for hints and clues of a second round on the horizon.

Over the next few months, the executives tried to conduct business as usual. Signs came, one after another, and were noted by the more veteran workers. After fourteen years in the industry, I knew the routine subtleties of layoffs. I could read the signs like sailors read the weather. Not wanting to be caught in the crosshairs, I started saving money.

Then the market crashed and angel investor money dried up completely. Our product wasn't bringing in sufficient revenue to justify the monthly burn rate. My internal alarm sounded—the end was coming. When I asked my boss if I had anything to worry about, he skirted a direct answer, saying that he hadn't been told anything yet. It was one more sign.

On the morning of January 12th, 2001, I logged onto my computer and an email flashed across the screen—"Mandatory Company Conference Call! 11:00 a.m. sharp. All employees must attend!" More layoffs! I was a director, and I hadn't been notified. I began packing up my things.

Once again, people congregated in the game room outside of their offices. This time, I went out to join them. We were all in the same boat now. The mood was grim, and fear-laden faces filled the room. I engaged with my staff and the other engineers, trying to stay calm. No one could work, so we passed the time playing foosball on the table I'd bought the year before.

Shortly before 11:00 a.m. I returned to my desk to wait for the call. The thought flashed through my mind—*Maybe I'll be kept on*. But I wasn't hopeful.

My phone rang and I reluctantly answered. "Cindy, please come up to the CEO's office." My manager's voice was somber.

I walked up the short flight of stairs, churning with anxiety, and entered the open door. I sat down in the only empty chair opposite the CEO's desk. My manager sat a few feet away. Their faces were grim masks; I could see this wasn't easy for them, either.

I'd been preparing for this day for months, but I wasn't prepared for what happened next. Not only was I laid off, but my entire department—all the people who had worked so hard with me over the past four years—were being laid off, as well.

My first response was my default; I took it personally. And my brain raced with catastrophic thoughts. "How can they do this? I worked so hard for them! We all did! What is my team going to do? It isn't fair! They could have given me a heads-up, but they hid it for months! What am I going to do? I have a daughter to raise! What if I can't find another job?"

This flurry of reactive thoughts was accompanied by a flood of reactive emotions—despair, anger, fear, resentment, and self-pity. I was in shock.

I sat still for a moment, listening within for the whispers of higher Soul perspectives hidden behind these frantic reactions, like the sun hidden behind storm clouds.

Then I made a shift that expanded my view. I took my focus off my reactive thoughts and emotions and looked at the two men I had worked with and come to respect and appreciate over the previous four years. I felt the sadness hidden behind their somber faces. I put myself in their place and empathized with their predicament. And my thoughts and feelings changed.

"I'm so sorry," I told them sincerely. "You've both worked so hard to build this company. It must be difficult to lay off all these people."

The energy in the room shifted. Their bodies relaxed. Instead of dismissing me, they opened up to me with a sense of relief, and we had a heartfelt conversation. They told me the full story they'd been keeping to themselves for months, and I could see how much it had burdened them.

After listening intently, I truly understood, and I accepted this outcome. They'd had no other choice. They'd kept people on for as long as they possibly could. When I left the building with my things that afternoon, I gifted my foosball table to the remaining engineers from the surviving teams.

MEANING IN CHAOS

Unemployed, at home, and living on a small severance, I often reflected on the layoffs, remembering how I had made a shift and handled the situation gracefully. I felt good about that, but it was hard to maintain my trust and optimism day to day, moment to moment. The layoff unleashed recurring doubts and fears that often disrupted my sense of wellbeing, and at times I reached panic levels.

My situation was dire. Almost everything seemed out of control. Yet, I knew I had two options: succumb to the fear or choose to shift my perspective and expand my consciousness in the face of these difficult emotions and my uncertain situation. I chose the second option. I frequently asked myself, "What is the positive lesson in all of this?"

And deep in my mind a mantra continually played: "Keep on keeping on."

I knew that *how* I handled the situation mattered more than the situation itself. The only thing I could control was how I *interpreted* it and how I *responded* to it. And this would be decisive. This was where the game would be won or lost.

By choice, I became my own coach. I practiced listening to my Soul's wise council rather than my fear-based personality's doom and gloom prophecies. I continually reminded myself that my Soul required this situation for my spiritual growth and evolution. Life wasn't dropping me into an abyss; it was moving me forward. This wasn't an end; it was a transition.

I rigorously trained myself to catch my fears as they arose, especially in moments of panic, and to recognize the negative thoughts that fed my fears and replace them with Soul thoughts that supported action and nourished hope. I knew that this job ending meant there was something better out there for me. So, I visualized myself conducting a job search with feelings of trust and contentment. I programmed my mind with clear intention and affirmed: *I am walking through the door at the first day of my new job!*

All this didn't happen easily. It was arduous work that required passion and conviction. I had to constantly remember and choose to practice, especially in difficult moments when I felt like collapsing in fear or bursting into tears. I felt like an elite athlete training for a championship game.

The more I practiced, the more I chose trust over fear, the stronger and more hopeful I felt, and the easier and more natural it became. The more I let go and believed in a higher plan, the more this seemingly disastrous situation was revealed as a blessing in disguise.

My loss of employment turned out to be much needed and invaluable time off, even a kind of spiritual retreat. It was "just what the doctor ordered." I spent the year learning, trusting, persevering, and growing. I found ways to make ends meet. I reignited my meditation practice and built a mindfulness routine of observing and releasing all of my negative default thoughts and emotions.

Not surprisingly, when the right time came, the universe worked its magic and provided a miracle. I found a great job. Within a year, I was promoted and began receiving more money and recognition than I'd ever expected.

Looking back, I can honestly say that I did a good job handling it all. No matter how many times I failed or despaired, I continued to practice with the situation and exercise my Soul. I didn't do it perfectly, but I did it sincerely to the best of my ability. That's all that is required of any of us. It's all we can do. And it's enough.

GROWTH POTENTIAL

That year of intense practice in the face of uncertainty and seeming powerlessness strengthened my connection to my Soul and to the higher powers that have always guided my life. In the face of these ongoing setbacks and uncertainties, I found a place of freedom inside me, like the proverbial calm eye in a hurricane. I found the tools to deepen my faith and master my fears while taking practical steps to move forward on my path. The growth I achieved, the lessons I learned, and the skills I acquired could not have come any other way.

We all yearn for freedom, peace, and contentment. But we only develop these qualities by wrestling with the inevitable difficulties and challenges of life. For example, does this sound like you?

"How will I ever make enough money to live a good life?"

"Now that my husband has passed away, will I ever get along without him?"

"Going to college is so hard these days. How am I ever going to write a meaningful personal essay that stands out?"

"I am not sure how to maintain peace of mind when someone hurts me or lashes out at me, it's so painful!"

These challenging situations can overwhelm you with fear or become Soul-stirring opportunities for growth—Soul food that nourishes you. In times of struggle and hardship, you can escape paralyzing lower thought-waves of your personality by shifting to higher perspectives that communicate the wisdom of your Soul—you can choose between automatic personality responses and conscious Soul choices.

The subtle choices you make in the struggles of life either limit or expand (exercise) your Soul. So, when difficulties and challenges come, identify the emotion you're feeling and turn within. Listen for the voice of your Soul that lets you see the bigger picture and grasp the higher meanings beyond the limited vision and reach of your personality. Ask yourself, "What is a higher perspective, the positive emotion, and the growth potential in this situation?"

If you do this over and over, no matter what life brings you or how many times you seemingly fail, you'll develop a habit of seeking and finding your Soul's guidance in all situations. You'll develop and deepen a conscious relationship with your Soul as it leads you through the emotional turbulence of life to your greater goal. This is what *Soulercise* is all about. This is your higher life purpose.

CHAPTER 2

Soul & Personality

"You don't have a Soul. You are a Soul. You have a body."
—Buddha

Whether we realize it or not, our planet is a multi-dimensional training ground, and we are spiritual warriors, masters in training, angels in process. Every morning we may wake up thinking we're simply going to school, to work, to the store, or to any other "ordinary" activity. But every moment, every step, every challenge, crisis and setback, every situation and event, inside and out, is part of our curriculum in the school of life designed to strengthen our spirit, awaken wisdom, and enlighten our being.

This is why so many Souls enter the Earth plane.

Do you realize how precious your time and experiences on Earth truly are? Do you know that the most difficult events and circumstances—the challenges, conflicts, crises, and traumas you resist and do everything to avoid—are the essential conditions and catalysts for your spiritual growth?

Do you know how much you will appreciate and value these transformative events when you complete this life and cross over to the other side, if not sooner?

Your ability to see them in this light, through the eyes of your Soul, as they bear down on you, dissolves ignorance and solidifies the nature of your higher self. It increases your capacity to rise above the onslaught of frantic thoughts and raging emotions they stir up in you and merge with divine states of compassion, empathy, and joy to live wisely and effectively from the essence of your being.

When you pass from this life you will know and measure your victory not by the values of your Earth-bound personality, but by the values of your Soul. You will understand that how you treated yourself and others; whether you grew emotionally and spiritually; whether you based your life in trust or fear; whether you succeeded or failed to take advantage of the opportunities for growth that your life presented, were far more important than the job you had, the money you made, the car you drove, the worldly status you achieved, or the earthly pleasures you experienced.

CHOICES

In every moment you have choices to make—what to eat, think, say, wear, or do next. Your choices may be intentional or automatic, practical or spiritual, mundane or life-altering. We all make subtle default choices all the time, unaware that we're choosing or that we have a choice at all.

These choices include the trains of thought you board many times a day; the feelings and emotions you gravitate toward, succumb to, and feed with your attention; the ingrained perspectives you use to analyze and assess people and circumstances; and your automatic and spontaneous reactions in any given moment.

Beyond and prior to these subtle choices lies a deeper, forgotten choice every Soul here has made—to enter the Earth plane, incarnate in a physical body, and attend the school of life on Earth.

My own trauma-induced out-of-body experience authenticates the assertion of many spiritual teachers that before we enter this material world we sit in an "all-knowing" state with the Beings of Light and carefully chart our Soul plan in detail; that we choose the events, experiences and relationships that will help us master our specific emotions and evolve as a Soul in our relatively brief sojourn on Earth.

But soon after birth we forget our previous existence and the Soul chart we created. At times, we may wonder why our life seems so difficult. We may find ourselves wishing that it were easier, that we could find a way out, or even wishing that we'd never been born.

I was born breech (butt first), and I've laughed at the idea that maybe, as I was about to enter the Earth school, my "curriculum" flashed before me and I panicked, turned around, and tried to go back. *"Wait! What was I thinking? Hold the presses, let's rethink this!"* But there was no turning back.

Consider that you willingly chose to come here, to take on every challenge and learn every lesson required for your spiritual development. Consider that you came here fully prepared, equipped, and determined to succeed.

You were also born vulnerable, helpless, and unable to fend for yourself. Over time, this changes and progresses, but as it does, life can often become overwhelming, confusing, and painful. And success doesn't come easy.

But you chose your life situations for a specific purpose. Your Soul mentors you and works through your personality while on Earth to accomplish your goals. Best of all, you are equipped with everything you need to conquer all of the challenges and tragedies you may face in life and to evolve into higher states of being.

Now that's good news!

PERSONALITY

Webster's dictionary defines the personality as "a complex of thoughts, emotions and behaviors that distinguishes an individual's characteristic patterns." Many factors contribute to form these patterns, including your time and date of birth, your cultural background, your parents, family members, teachers, friends, and life experiences.

Through all of this, beliefs are programmed in your subconscious about yourself and "the way things are." These hidden beliefs shape your personality and influence how you perceive, think about, react to, and are impacted by the people and events in your life.

Psychologist Carl Jung not only described the soul/psyche as a repository of virtually limitless potential for growth and transformation, but he also saw that this process of growth and transformation occurs through the vehicle of our personality as it grapples with and integrates its life experiences. And to illuminate this process of personality transformation, he used the alchemical metaphor of changing a base substance into a valuable substance— "turning lead into gold."

Your personality's behavioral/psychological patterns are shaped and programed by your total life environment; by all that you experience and feel, are told or taught; by the beliefs you form and the meanings you make out of all these things; and especially by the people in your life.

You may have "learned" that you were "good" or "bad," "smart" or "stupid," "pretty" or "plain," a poor sport, a great athlete, a nerd, ADHD, or fill in the blank. Your parents may have taught you to "eat properly," "speak politely," "behave," "be good," and know the difference between right and wrong.

They may also, due to their own difficult childhoods, have failed to adequately meet the challenges and fulfill the obligations of parenthood. Maybe they imposed on you their expectations and their vision of who you "ought to be," or took their frustrations out on you through judgments, criticism, punishment, neglect, or by withholding love.

To earn your parents' approval or love, or to avoid criticism and punishment, you may have internalized their expectations, learned to see yourself through their eyes, and tried to be who you thought they wanted you to be.

Formative childhood events, conditions, and traumas impact each of us. The thoughtless or cruel words and actions of others, and even their innocent mistakes, can feel like poisonous darts or devastating blows. They can unleash powerful storms of thought and emotion that muddle our clarity and impair our self-control.

All these things and more etch pain and trauma into our neural patterns. They skew our perceptions, shape our perspectives, and form deep-seated subconscious beliefs hidden from view.

These beliefs function as hidden automatic programs that frame our interpretations of our experiences and affect how we relate to ourselves and the world. They can trigger digestive problems and other troubling health issues. But most importantly, they cause us to lose touch with our authentic selves.

We all experience some of these things to some degree. We all have automatic subconscious thoughts and beliefs that influence and affect us; that generate disturbing feelings, painful emotions, and consume our vital energy.

Such negative beliefs and thoughts are often linked to recurring sadness, depression, fear, anger, sorrow, or doubt.

"I'm too fat."

"I have nothing to offer."

"I'm not smart/good enough."

"I feel so alone."

Such beliefs and the negative emotions they trigger can prevent us from finding the love, acceptance, compassion, and meaning we crave.

But you don't have to settle for this. You can recognize and disarm limiting, painful, self-destructive beliefs about yourself, others, and the world that hold you back and keep you from fulfilling your purpose.

With enough awareness, commitment, willpower and energy, you can unveil your hidden belief systems and build thoughts and emotions that work for you rather than against you. You can transform fear, doubt, anger, or any negative emotions that may characterize your personality into their higher vibrational counterparts. You can turn "lead into gold!" And, in doing so, you cultivate the strength to liberate your true self from the bondage of dysfunctional conditioning.

But few of us were raised to believe in the unlimited energy and possibility that lie within us. Most of us were taught and conditioned to perceive and live solely as separate personalities in a limited reality.

We weren't told that by filling up and tapping into our inner reservoir, we can align with our Soul and become sources of strength, compassion, empathy, and love to ourselves and to the people in our lives, and serve as beacons in the world, lighting the way for others.

SOUL

Webster's dictionary defines the Soul as "the spiritual part of a person that is believed to give life to the body, and in many religions, is believed to live forever."

The Soul is the origin of all profound insights and spiritual perceptions. When the personality perceives these insights and perceptions, it can choose, of its own free will, to apply them or not. It is also the origin of all true spiritual and religious teachings. When the personality encounters these teachings, it can also choose, of its own free will, to live by them or not.

The Soul is the Holy Grail, the mystical repository of the Sacred. It is the Philosopher's Stone that turns the "lead" of personality consciousness into the "gold" of Soul consciousness. It is "Brahman," the universal cosmic Soul, or eternal life Source, of which the individual Soul or "Atman" is intricately a part. Because of this, conscious, personality-transforming Soul contact is the global goal of true spiritual and religious teachings.

For millennia, almost every culture and spiritual tradition in the world has acknowledged the Soul as an integral component of man, but in the manic hustle and bustle of modern life, the Soul can seem hidden, out of reach, or like a fairy tale. Although the Soul is non-physical, it is as real as your body and requires equal attention and care. It is your core self in the spiritual dimension, residing within you now.

A conscious relationship with your Soul opens access to higher energy frequencies and spiritual guidance beyond the range of your conditioned personality. It is a vital component and the essential foundation of a spiritual life.

In recent decades, awareness and reverence for the Soul has been growing. More of us than ever before want to know our Soul and enhance our connection to higher realms. We want to access wisdom and peace and find sanctuary amidst the instability of our stress-filled lives.

The good news is that when we are present in the moment and pay attention to our thoughts and reactions without judgement, the divine emerges within us. A source of wisdom, peace, and sanctity comes forward, and the non-physical, eternal aspect of our being—our Soul—shines its light within and even through our limited and conditioned personality into higher realms.

The other good news is that we are not alone on this journey. The moment we decide to enter the challenging training ground of incarnation, our Soul, along with our spiritual teachers, becomes our ally and guide on our evolutionary path.

When life gets complicated, we naturally look for help and answers everywhere outside of us in the world around us. That's important, but we can't neglect to also turn to the Beings of Light and to look in the one place where the Soul wisdom we seek truly resides—within our *own* being.

Developing a relationship with your Soul means "going within." Just like exercise, it requires the consistent, ongoing commitment and free will effort of your personality. This consistent commitment and free will effort to contact and "hear" your Soul is a personality-transforming spiritual practice that over time allows you to actually maintain the peace of meditation in the "heart of life," even in the midst of challenging situations.

SOUL GROWTH

Your individual Soul is a vibrational essence descending into the lower vibrations of the Earth to inhabit a physical form with a specific Soul plan. When your life plan is ready, and the positions of the sun, moon, and planets are synchronized with the content of your individual blueprint, your Soul enters the Earth plane.

Because the moment of your birth is an astrological snapshot of your blueprint, understanding your astrology/Vedic astrology helps you understand who you are now (your personality) and who you want to become (your Soul). It tells you most of what you need to know about your Soul blueprint—why you are here and what your Soul purpose is in this lifetime.

The diagram on the next page illustrates how consciousness descends into the lower vibrations of Earth, inhabits a physical body, and takes on a personality. It depicts your Soul as a being of light energy that comes to Earth with a plan designed to teach, challenge, and test you.

It also introduces the notion of "Soul growth" and shows how your Soul plan details the situations and challenging emotions you will experience. And it shows that, as you learn from the events of your life over time, you grow and evolve into higher vibrational states, even into spiritual realms beyond the material worlds.

To fulfill your growth potential and master your Soul plan you must come to know your *whole* self—from the patterns and programs of your conditioned personality to the power and wisdom of your Soul.

Once in your Earth body, your Soul and your personality exist simultaneously but vibrate at different rates. Your Soul's higher vibrations connect it to Source.

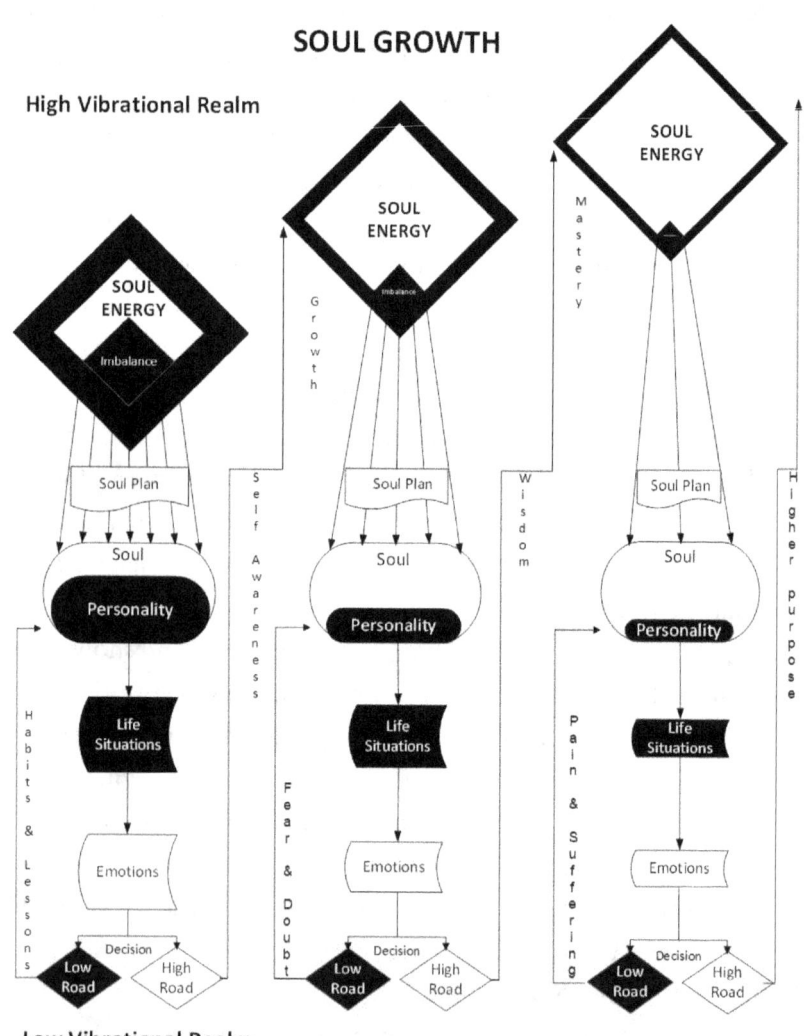

Your personality is connected to the body, which is a kind of anchor for the Soul in the Earth plane. You make the most of this lifetime by striving to bring your personality into perfect alignment with your Soul.

This Soul alignment occurs as the personality is tested and refined in the fires of life experiences, and increasingly transforms its lower "negative" thoughts, emotions, and energies into higher "positive" ones.

As you transform your lower emotions and thinking patterns into their higher Soul counterparts, you raise your personality's vibrational rate, and it increasingly harmonizes and merges with your Soul.

As your Soul functions more powerfully within you and in the world around you, its radiant, healing light increasingly shines through you into the human realm. You access an increasing awareness, clarity, and wisdom often called "enlightenment," and your Soul progressively evolves into higher vibrational states of being.

If this sounds daunting or complicated, just remember this simple truth: The most powerful choice you can make in any moment is to turn to and live by the highest power in the universe that thrives and shines within you.

Only this power can lead you unerringly along the path of your higher purpose and guide you to consistently make choices that strengthen rather than weaken you, that heal rather than harm you (and others), that expand your consciousness and move you forward in your evolution. And as you continually utilize this inexhaustible source of wisdom and renewal over time, you establish a new foundation for living.

So, exercise your Soul every day in every situation; in prayer, meditation, sports, work, and service to others; in resolving misunderstandings and conflicts; in enjoying good company, communing with nature, or performing any of the countless tasks life requires of you.

Consciously coach yourself—with the same dedication and drive that you would bring to improving at your favorite sport, building your career, or maintaining a fit and healthy body—to go higher and deeper within. Learn to see through your personality's limited thoughts and reactions and to discern your Soul's higher wisdom. Then make the light and truths of your Soul your guiding compass on the field of life.

Every situation you encounter is a spiritual opportunity to practice being who and what you want to become during your brief sojourn on Earth. So, when life's difficult challenges and tests trigger negative thoughts and emotions, look through them into the spiritual dimension and bring light into the darkness by calling on the power of your Soul. Affirm: *I am transforming this situation as a spiritual warrior, with higher thoughts that generate love, compassion, and strength!*

If you do this over time, you'll not only live life as a being of light on Earth, but also evolve into higher vibrational realms of spirit beyond the Earth; beyond the need to reincarnate in a physical body in a material world. You'll graduate from the school of life to a higher purpose on a higher plane.

This is the essence of *Soulercise*.

CHAPTER 3

Thoughts are Things

"To say a thing 'must be' is the very power that makes it"
—Prentice Mulford, *Thoughts Are Things*

We've all heard that "like attracts like," and "birds of a feather flock together." You may even have heard that "thoughts are things," a phrase coined by Prentice Mulford in 1890. But what do these sayings mean? Do mysterious vibrations influence our lives, emanate from our thoughts, draw us to things, and things to us, based on matching vibrations? And if so, can these vibrations eventually be measured, and tools invented to utilize them?

The x-ray machine and the radio, both invented near the turn of the 20th century, harnessed the invisible forces of electromagnetic radiation and radio waves that had always existed.

In 1939, Semyon Kirlian, using inventive photographic techniques, accidently photographed invisible electrical discharges, revealing a radiant light emanating from all living things now known as Kirlian Photography.

MRIs and CAT Scans use x-rays combined with sophisticated computers to view with unprecedented detail the organs in the body, otherwise undetectable to us. EEGs can record the invisible electrical impulses and chemical activities in the brain.

We know that certain sounds and colors, electrical waves, and cosmic rays exist beyond the range of human perception because technology now exists to measure them. We know that the Earth's magnetic field makes a continuous complex sound we cannot hear that scientists call a chorus, because satellites can now orbit the Earth and record it.

So, do our thought waves travel through space like radio waves and electromagnetic waves and energetically affect plants, animals, and other human beings? Do these thought waves affect us physically, emotionally, sub-atomically? What other vibratory forms of energy exist that we currently lack the technology to measure? And how might these energetic phenomena affect and influence us without our awareness?

THOUGHT VIBRATION

Einstein's equation, $E=MC2$, shattered our ideas about the nature of reality, about time and space, and about the substance of things. His discovery about the nature of light, energy, and matter was world changing. Simply put: Light is energy, and energy is light.

This light/energy can vibrate at various frequencies. At low enough vibrational frequencies, light/energy coalesces into matter—the lower the vibrational frequency, the denser the matter. So, all matter of any density—whether cotton, wood, diamond, or steel—is only vibrating light/energy.

Differing light/energy frequencies also produce variations in colors; red, orange, and yellow at one end of the spectrum, and green, blue, violet, and white at the other end. It's the same with ranges of pitch or sound—high and low, soft and loud; and with degrees of temperature—hot and cold.

There is also a vibrational frequency spectrum that cannot be seen with the eye but can be measured with technology—infrared and radio waves at the low end, and ultra-violet, x-rays, and gamma rays at the high end.

Thanks to scientists like Einstein, we can harness various forms of invisible energy, such as electricity and electromagnetic frequencies, for use in our daily lives. And today, scientists are working to harness the power of thought (also a form of light/energy) to operate technologies that will benefit millions of people.

Former Army Staff Sgt. Glen Lehman, who lost is right arm in Baghdad in 2008, can now manipulate his prosthetic arm and hand to grab, lift, write and more, using the electromagnetic impulses generated by his thoughts.

Barbara Eldredge writes of this new thought-directed technology now benefitting upper-limb amputees: "A team of doctors and military researchers have developed a way to tap directly into neural impulses sent from the brain to the hands. Should this technology reach the mainstream, we won't need keyboards, computer mice, or touch screens. We won't, as in Glen Lehman's case, need biological hands at all."

THOUGHT WAVE EFFECTS

Approximately 50,000 thoughts and/or images pass through the average person's mind each day. Studies show that every image, thought, and feeling passing through our mind triggers complex biochemical processes in the body and stimulates millions of neuronal connections in the brain. If thoughts generate energetic waves or impulses that can operate technologies and manipulate matter, it is reasonable to believe they also affect us, others, and the world around us.

The fact that positive and negative thoughts have a corresponding effect on our moods and energy levels supports the idea that positive and negative thoughts have higher and lower vibrational frequencies that positively or negatively affect our health and the quality of our lives.

In the book *Buddha's Brain*, psychologist Rick Hanson and neuroscientist Richard Mendius describe how synapses in our brain that fire frequently become more sensitive, and how our experiences and thoughts promote the growth of new synapses and can even change our genes and alter the structure of our brain. As the authors put it, "the brain takes its shape from what the mind rests upon."

In other words, if we repeatedly entertain thoughts and feelings with similar vibrational frequencies, we carve neural pathways or "connections" in our brain that can increase their recurrence and make them habitual. This is good if we choose **higher vibrational thoughts and feelings like love, joy, serenity, compassion, humor, etc.**

This is illustrated in the "Thought Wave Effect" chart on the opposite page.

Lower thoughts—anger, jealousy, and fear—deplete our energy, lower our vibrational frequency, and attract or draw us to people and situations vibrating at similar frequencies. Lower vibrational thoughts also eclipse the inspiring and rejuvenating thoughts and presence of our Soul, depleting our life force and negatively affecting our health and relationships.

Soul qualities—patience, trust, and love—energize us, raise our vibrational frequency, and connect us to the positive forces

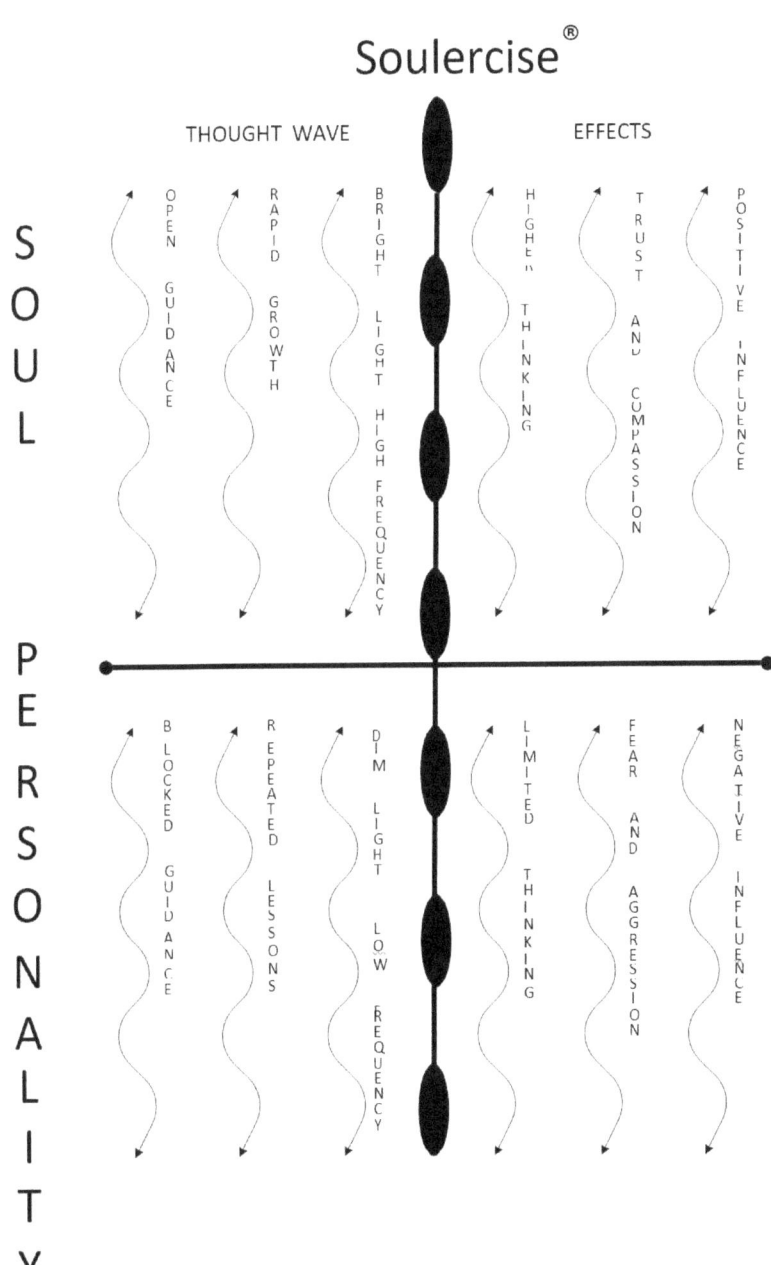

in the universe vibrating at similar frequencies. Such higher thoughts and feelings raise our consciousness and light/energy frequency, strengthen our life force, and positively impact our life circumstances, our health, and our relationships.

QUALITY OF LIFE

Your personality and your Soul generate energy frequencies that affect you and radiate into the world around you. Your thoughts and emotions not only affect your vibrational frequency and your consciousness, but they also affect the people around you, your access to material resources on the Earth plane, and to transcendent resources beyond the material world.

So, it's important to choose, consciously and wisely, at the initiatory level of your thoughts, those of a higher vibrational frequency, for they affect the course and quality of your life in many ways.

When negative thoughts and perspectives attract negative experiences, these experiences reinforce your thoughts and then attract more negative experiences. This repetitive negativity becomes a vicious cycle. The neural pathways it carves in your brain foster habitual negative patterns that dominate your consciousness and affect every aspect of your being and every area of your life.

Because "like attracts like," if you hold on to lower vibrational negative thoughts, you will attract or gravitate to people and situations vibrating at similar low-energy frequencies. You will choose them because they feel familiar and more comfortable, whether they're good for you or not. And because people and situations vibrating at higher vibrational frequencies will feel uncomfortable and unfamiliar, you will tend to unconsciously avoid or shy away from them.

Thoughts Are Things

Over time, you become accustomed to the negative, lower-vibrational thoughts of your conditioned personality. They feel normal even when they're stressful or cause problems. It is common for negative thoughts to eventually become a habit you unconsciously gravitate towards as you continually agonize about the past or worry about the future.

It's also common to automatically create stories around your reactive thoughts that you believe to be the only truth. But you have a choice in the matter, you can change the channel.

The thoughts you embrace reflect and reinforce your present level of consciousness. Habitual negative thoughts not only diminish the quality of your life and your light/energy frequency, but also the power and effectiveness of your actions, the amount of assistance available to you from above, and the speed at which you move forward in your evolution. They block your intuitive access to the deeper insights and guidance of your Soul and keep you from fulfilling your higher purpose in this lifetime.

So, will you continue to live by the limits of your conditioned personality? Or will you choose to tune in to the wisdom of your Soul and apply its liberating insights to improve the quality of your life?

One of my challenges in this lifetime is to tune in to channels broadcasting thoughts of trust and confidence when overcome by negativity around sickness and death. I chose to be born with my younger sister Debby who, at the age of ten, suffered a life-threatening illness. I was only twelve years old at the time when Debby was whisked away to Children's Hospital Los Angeles.

We are extremely close, and I was devasted when my parents told me she was going to die. For months Debby lived in isolation while doctors worked to manage her illness with a newly introduced treatment of corticosteroids. She was among one of the first groups of people to be diagnosed with Lupus.

While my dad was at work, my mom spent most of her days at the hospital with Debby. I went to stay with my godparents who lived a couple of blocks from our house. During this time, I rarely spoke to my parents. Our main contact was after-school check-in phone calls. I never knew from one day to the next if Debby would survive. Alone and isolated by fear and anxiety, I withdrew from friends, acted out at times with reckless abandon, and often had problems at school.

Debby was eventually released from the hospital but returned off and on for years when her Lupus flared up. Our family jokes now that Debby was hospitalized so many times that she outgrew the beds at Children's Hospital Los Angeles. But at the time, I didn't know how to cope with the ongoing trauma. I didn't know that I was continually reinforcing and magnifying my feelings of fear and insecurity by the stories I told myself.

When crying didn't help anymore, I remembered how praying had saved me the night my grandmother died. So, I started praying for Debby. I started praying for the strength to bear everything that was happening and for help to understand the magnitude of my experience. Prayer became a lifeline. It helped me to think positive thoughts and find comfort. It helped me to let go and feel a sense of calm in a storm of negativity.

When I succumbed to my negative thoughts, the resulting fear became my signal to pray. Prayer opened me up to a greater power that I could trust when life seemed completely untrustworthy. It gave me increasing access to a mysterious source of contentment within me. And I noticed that as I continued a practice of prayer, the quality of my life improved. Doors opened for me, and people and resources arrived as needed.

In every moment we all have these choices to make. And with enough commitment, effort, and awareness, you can choose to find freedom from the emotions your negative thoughts evoke and improve the quality of your life. You can form new habits of enlightened thinking that carve optimal neural pathways in your brain and align your personality with the higher vibrations of your Soul.

As your inner light and outlook on life brighten, you'll be drawn to people and situations with similar higher vibrational frequencies. And you'll experience a renewed sense of trust in life and inspiration from within.

THOUGHT BROADCASTS

We are each a vibrational light/energy transmission station. Every moment of every day we are broadcasting between a range of high frequency, positive, wise thoughts and low frequency, negative, irrational thoughts. To those mostly broadcasting denser lower-vibrating negative thoughts, the automatic reactions of the personality are naturally louder than the insightful, enlightening voice of the Soul.

However, during any challenging situation, a simple practice of tuning in to higher Soul thoughts and emotions refines your listening, clarifies your consciousness, and raises your vibrational level. As you raise your vibrational level, your Soul's wisdom broadcasts become stronger and louder, easier to hear, and easier to follow. And your old reactive thoughts and emotions diminish in power and fade into the background.

So, practice in every situation. Be mindful of your thoughts, the emotions they generate, the vibrations they emanate, and the effects they have on you and others. Observe the inner broadcast of your habitual thoughts, feelings, and patterns of behavior. Observe how you interpret and respond to others and situations in your life.

Do you interpret challenges and crises as negative events and react to them from a place of anger, fear, or despair? If so, practice seeing them from your Soul's wisdom perspective, as lessons life is teaching you and opportunities for further growth and evolution. Practice responding to them with thoughts that generate trust, courage, and optimism.

When you fail or make a mistake, do you judge or criticize yourself for what you did wrong, or dwell on what you should have done instead? If so, practice supporting and encouraging yourself like a true friend. Reflect on and learn from your experience. Keep moving forward, choosing thoughts that build trust in life; perspectives that generate faith in yourself and your ultimate success.

When people say or do things that hurt you, do you let angry thoughts consume you? If so, the next time you are hurt, call on the light and presence of your Soul. Remember that everyone makes mistakes in life, and that you've hurt others in the past. Let go of your hurtful thoughts and forgive others for being human, just like you.

Do you struggle alone with challenges and problems? Do you feel reluctant, unworthy, or perhaps too proud to ask others for help? Do you let your thoughts and fears guide you in a crisis, as if no higher spiritual help is available? If so, practice releasing your fearful thoughts. Reach out to people you trust. Be open to receive guidance and inspiration that are always available from professionals near you and in the Universe surrounding you.

Turn in faith to your Soul and to your Higher Power as you understand it. Make self-mastery and Soul growth your daily practice and your higher purpose. The 7 Soulercise Steps will show you how. They will guide you to transform your thought broadcasts with the light, power, and presence of your Soul perspectives.

If you do this, you will build bridges to your Soul and clarity, trust, confidence, and joy will become the dominant expressions of your being. And your outer life will reflect your inner transformation. As you use life's tests and challenges as opportunities for your Soul's evolution, you grow in self-knowledge, self-mastery, and you fulfill your higher purpose.

Life will continue to challenge you to grow beyond your present state. But your relationship to life, with all of its problems, will become increasingly based in trust and filled with meaning. People will respond to you differently. Some will be drawn to you and be inspired and uplifted by you. And you will become an angel of light, even as you walk on the Earth in a physical body.

CHAPTER 4

States of Emotion

*"For every minute you are angry
you lose sixty seconds of happiness."*

—Ralph Waldo Emerson

Your higher purpose is not *fulfilled* in worldly pursuits, but in mastering your thoughts and emotions, which either bind you within the limitations of your personality or open you up to the healing presence and consciousness of your Soul. Indeed, Soul growth is why you came into this life on Earth, but exactly how do you consciously attain self-mastery and ensure that you accomplish what you came here to do?

The short answer is......you identify the contents of your Soul plan. You recognize both the lower emotions that *consume* you and the higher emotions that *free* you. When you identify the specific emotions that drive you, you will know exactly what you planned to master in this life.

States of Emotion

AN OPPORTUNITY TO GROW

Negative thoughts trigger negative emotions and vice versa. In a world full of challenges, it's vitally important to become aware of not only the kind of thoughts you tend to think around a given situation, but also the emotion your thoughts and/or situation is generating. Only then can you do the inner work required to transform them.

I experienced the reality of this when I was nineteen years old. Still in Los Angeles, I was preparing to attend a small college in England with my first love, Christopher, who had at the last minute communicated he wanted to "just be friends."

Devastated, I decided to buy a new spiritual book to take with me. I went to Pickwick Bookshop on Hollywood Blvd. and immediately headed for the self-help section. There, I saw Mick Jagger and his first wife Bianca browsing through the aisles.

Being a Mick Jagger fan, but not wanting to bother them, I casually moved past the shelves until I came to their aisle. As I stood there, pretending to browse, watching them out of the corner of my eye, a book fell off a nearby shelf a few feet away. I went over and picked it up. The title read *Freedom from the Known* by J. Krishnamurti.

I closed my eyes, opened the book to a random page, and read a small section of the text. Krishnamurti's words struck to the core of my being. It read: "One of our greatest difficulties is to see for ourselves really clearly, not only outward things but inward life."

Intrigued with the idea of "seeing inward life," I didn't even notice Mick and Bianca leave the store.

Living in an old English Monastery in England and in close quarters with Christopher, having to just be friends with the one I loved was an exceptional challenge. *Freedom from the Known* became a kind of personal Bible, and Krishnamurti became my teacher.

Krishnamurti taught me how to do the inner work of transformation—how to find freedom from my sadness and how to bring the light of my higher self into the darkness of my unconscious, conditioned self. My traumatic break up turned out to be a life-changing "opportunity" for growth and Soul transformation, thanks to an enlightened philosopher from India.

Your emotional states are mirrors reflecting who you are choosing to be in any moment. They tell you when you are on the path that leads you into greater harmony, or greater conflict, with yourself and those around you.

As you can see from the "Emotion List" on the opposite page, every emotion you feel is a lower/negative challenge with a higher transformational opportunity. Every habitual thought either perpetuates a challenging personality emotion like fear, anger, and insecurity, or a supportive Soul emotion like trust, peace, and confidence.

All lower/negative, often personality-driven emotions are opportunities for Soul growth and can be resolved by affirming and living their higher/positive counterparts. Every time you choose the wiser perspectives of your Soul, you increase your emotional wellbeing and your growth opportunities.

Perhaps you didn't get the job you wanted or get into the college of your choice. Perhaps the relationship you were in didn't work out, or the parents you have aren't present or supportive and you, too, are dealing with the pain of loss and rejection.

The lower emotions triggered by your life situation can only be resolved in the higher Soul state of acceptance and understanding. So, the baseline goal in *Soulercising* is to transform your lower

States of Emotion

EMOTION LIST

CHALLENGE	OPPORTUNITY
Anger	Peace
Sadness	Joy
Insecurity	Confidence
Jealousy	Security
Fear	Trust
Abandonment	Support
Worry	Calm
Shame	Respect
Hostility	Compassion
Hate	Love
Rejection	Acceptance
Depression	Gratitude
Apathy	Passion
Weakness	Strength
Doubt	Faith
Criticism	Approval
Disappointment	Satisfaction
Resentment	Forgiveness
Anxious	Relaxed
Timid	Proud
Frustration	Contentment

states of emotion into their higher states. And you do this by continually choosing the higher thought waves and emotions emanating from your Soul in the face of lower thoughts and emotions during difficult situations.

So, recognize experiences of loss and rejection as opportunities to grow by practicing acceptance and understanding until they become your reality in these circumstances. Recognize insecurity as an opportunity to develop confidence and stability. Recognize fear as an opportunity to develop trust. Recognize anger as an opportunity to cultivate stillness and inner calm.

As you *Soulercise* during difficult life events, you will become increasingly able to live in these higher emotional states as you fulfill your true mission here on Earth.

Understanding this provides a powerful context for living. You no longer see your emotions and experiences as random forces to struggle with, to try to repress or avoid. Recognizing their educational and transformative value, your goal now is to be transformed by them.

This context reveals the highest meaning and purpose of every situation and event, including financial setbacks, dysfunctional parents, severe illness, and even the death of a loved one. And this makes your life a self-fulfilling and Soul-fulfilling process.

The ability to live all of your experiences in the light of your Soul facilitates maximum spiritual growth. Instead of being trapped in limiting and self-defeating behavior patterns and life situations, *you work to find healthy and creative ways to express and channel the power of your emotions. You learn to keep an upbeat frame of mind as you creatively cope with the stress and painful emotions of life's problems and challenges.*

EMOTIONS & THE CHAKRAS

Mental, emotional, and psychological states produce positive and negative neurochemical changes in the body. Prolonged negative states can produce physical symptoms and illnesses. Carl Jung observed that every physical ailment has an emotional/psychological component. Whatever you feel at the level of personality, whether stuck in the throes of negative thoughts, or caught in the grip of lower emotional states, reverberates through, and affects, your body.

These reverberations can be felt palpably in your energy centers called chakras. The Sanskrit word chakra means "wheel." The chakras are nonphysical energy points or wheels of light in the human body. There are seven major chakras located on the spine between the perineum (or base) and the top of the head.

In many spiritual/energetic practices, you conduct energy and recharge your batteries or chakras. You draw energy from the universe into your body through the soles of your feet and the top of your head. This energy is distributed through your physical body and into your light body, called an aura.

Chakras also act like transformers by reducing the voltage of incoming energies to match your capacity to integrate them into your body/mind. Increase the energy capacity of each chakra and you raise the vibrational state/frequency in which you exist.

As every piano key corresponds to a specific note on a scale, so each Chakra corresponds to a note on the ancient Solfeggio scale, a six-tone sequence of electro-magnetic frequencies. The lower or base chakras vibrate at lower tones or frequencies, and the higher chakras vibrate at higher tones/frequencies.

If you focus your attention at each chakra, you can feel the "spinning wheel" energy sensation in that part of your body.

Lower emotional states like anger, fear, and anxiety vibrate in your lower chakras. And in these states, you conduct these lower vibrations in all that you do.

But when you shift from these lower personality states to higher Soul states, you conduct the energy of these higher chakras in all that you do. And that energy works in you and through you for your highest good and the highest good of all those you encounter.

So, wherever you are, in a grocery store, a business meeting, on a date, or just walking down the street, notice your emotional state and its corresponding energy vibration. If you notice a lower emotional state in the pit of your stomach, take a moment to prayerfully feel and activate your sixth or third eye chakra in your forehead.

This will help free you from the grip of any lower emotion and shift you to a higher Soul state of peace and compassion. Then you will recognize the opportunity and the higher purpose your situation is providing.

BROADCAST CHARTS

Since we are continually emitting waves of thought and subsequent emotions into a universe of things and beings all vibrating at different frequencies, whatever thoughts we choose become our reality. So, it is of the utmost importance to get to know the content of our radio broadcasts to ourselves, to others, and to the universe at large if we want to transform them.

Because our conditioned tendency is to subconsciously, and automatically, attach to low frequency (base level) personality thought waves, lower emotional states become our experiential reality and our primary channel. To transform these lower emotional states and change the channel to our Soul's perspective, we must get to know what both our personality and Soul thoughts are and how to find them.

Soulercise helps you to develop this skill, but you must put in the time and practice.

When you find yourself in a difficult situation and your emotions are getting the best of you, look at the thoughts you are automatically holding on to, identify the lower emotions they trigger or perpetuate in you, and *Soulercise* them into their higher Soul states.

This may not be easy in the beginning. So, it helps to build a Broadcast Chart that physically maps out your subconscious radio broadcasts—the inner dialogues associated with a given emotion—so you can change the channel if you are willing.

Your Broadcast Chart lays out the range of thoughts—from hidden lower personality thoughts to higher Soul thoughts—that difficult situations activate in you.

Using this tool helps you to clearly see the content of your thought broadcasts and identify the overriding emotion that those thoughts generate. It increases your ability to shift from subconscious identification with lower emotional states to conscious examination and awareness of those states. This develops self-awareness and, eventually, Soul awareness.

A good Broadcast Chart should map your habitual low frequency thoughts, the emotion surrounding them, and the ways that they leapfrog or escalate when self- and Soul-awareness are absent.

For example: When something happens that you don't like, you may automatically judge or blame yourself or others based on hidden subconscious programs. This can make you angry. It may stimulate in you a desire to lash out or a misguided need for revenge on others for their transgressions. This creates a downward spiral of negative thoughts, emotions, and behaviors that can cause unnecessary harm to you and to others.

When you unveil these hidden subconscious programs and personality thoughts in your Broadcast Chart, they will have less control over your emotional wellbeing. As you practice transforming them by tuning into your high frequency Soul thoughts and the emotions they generate, you increasingly emerge from the fog of fear and negativity that your personality broadcasts have created over the years.

The more you do this, the easier it becomes. With practice and repetition—no matter how many times you fail—you become more proficient at accessing the more subtle Soul broadcasts. As you master the art of shifting from your lower personality broadcast channel to your higher Soul broadcast channel, you become more balanced, peaceful, and effective in your life.

So, if you are having trouble in school, if you are stuck in a dead-end job, if you are coping with a serious illness, or you simply feel angry or frustrated with life, it's time to build a Broadcast Chart.

When your personality's subconscious programs are in control and your Soul's higher perspectives are faint glimmers in the darkness of emotional turmoil, a Broadcast Chart will reveal the scope of your automatic thoughts and amplify higher perspectives for you. Then you can make the switch and watch your life change for the better.

REVERSE ENGINEERING

Each Broadcast Chart you create for a particular emotional response to a challenging situation reveals some key element or diagram from the Soul plan you created before entering this lifetime.

As you progressively track your emotions through successive Broadcast Charts, you will notice there are key patterns of thoughts and emotions, actions and reactions that influence you. You will begin to see more clearly who you are and what you came here to work on. You reverse-engineer—you study, analyze, and learn the details of— the content of your Soul plan!

This is what the Beings of Light meant during my out-of-body experience when they told me, "In one mortal lifetime, you will attempt to master at the most two or three challenging emotions."

When you have consistently built several Broadcast Charts, you'll find that there are no new emotions, only new situations. You will see how the same set of emotions—and there is a finite number of them—repeat themselves through the people and situations in your life, continually challenging you to change the channel.

When you identify your specific set of emotions and own them as your lessons in this lifetime, you have a complete replica of your Soul Plan. And, most importantly, you discover your higher purpose.

But this doesn't have to be a grim, humorless affair. When a new and difficult situation presents itself, have fun catching your thoughts. Say to yourself, "Oh, there I go again, mindless thoughts, time to replace you—time to move this icky feeling up to my forehead!" When you can do this with lightheartedness, it makes the process fun.

So, when emotions get the best of you, remember to humor yourself when you struggle and celebrate when you succeed. Transforming emotional states can also become a passion, like excelling at your favorite computer game or achieving new levels of skill at your favorite sport.

Personality patterns, no matter how deeply ingrained, are no match for the light and power of your Soul. But it's up to you to consistently choose the one that transforms and liberates you, rather than the one that binds and limits you. So be patient with yourself. Get excited! You now have the knowledge and the tools to access the blueprint you designed for this lifetime and fulfill your higher purpose.

The more you practice and *Soulercise* the content of your thoughts and emotions, the more you build bridges to your Soul—automatically accessing its higher vibrations and radio broadcasts. As your Soul-alignment becomes more stable and old limiting patterns dissolve, your personality increasingly merges with your Soul, and your higher intuitive faculties awaken.

This in turn heightens your ability to also access the benign influences or broadcasts of the beings, teachers, and guides from the spirit realm; the unseen allies who bless and support you on your journey. Now that's exciting!

So, let's take a more in-depth look at the two Broadcast Realms and the 7 Steps to transforming life's challenges into opportunities for self-discovery and enlightenment.

CHAPTER 5

How to Soulercise

"Ask and it will be given to you; seek and you will find; knock and the door will be opened to you."

—Jesus

Since you chose the life circumstances, experiences, and even the physical body that would help you pursue your goals and support your maximum growth, you knew, prior to entering this lifetime, the weaknesses you would have. You knew the challenges and lessons you would face, the skills you would need to develop, and the accomplishments you intended to achieve.

You and your team of teachers profoundly considered and specifically designed all these things and more so you could fulfill your evolutionary potential. Then you arrived, prepared and motivated, but, again as we all do, promptly forgot everything you knew beforehand.

Once you are here, your task is to do your best to remember who you are in Spirit and stay on course, regardless of what happens. And you "stay on course" by managing your thoughts and emotions, maintaining a healthy, life-positive perspective, and doing the practical and spiritual work that transmutes raw Earthly experience into refined Soul consciousness.

All the above-mentioned factors are why sayings like "there are no accidents or coincidences," "everything happens for a reason," and even, "it's all good," are spiritually true, even when your life is difficult, traumatic, or even tragic in Earthly terms.

Recognizing yourself as the co-creator of your Soul plan takes you out of the personality consciousness of victimhood and puts you in the driver's seat of Soul consciousness. You can't control the flow of traffic on the highway of life, but you can learn to navigate effectively and achieve the goals you've set for yourself at each stage of your journey.

To a large extent, what you get out of life at any stage is your own creation; it's what you think and believe, deep down. Whatever comes to you or happens to you is, to a large extent, a result of the thoughts and perspectives you entertain, the words you speak, and the deeds you do.

So, what do you actually do when a negative situation occurs? What do you do if you feel rejected or betrayed; if you feel that your parents, siblings, spouse, or boss don't appreciate you; or if your loved one or family member is suffering a debilitating illness? How do you effectively manage your feelings and navigate through these difficult situations?

Books, classes, therapists, and friends can help you learn and grow in the school of life. But no matter how much you learn or know; you must do the work to evolve.

To begin, you examine yourself in the situation. You stop and listen to the thoughts you are repeatedly looping within. You embrace your thoughts and the feelings they generate and encourage yourself to find a new perspective on the situation. You take a few still moments to go within and hear higher thoughts also broadcasting within you.

Then you can do the necessary work to refine your attitude and positively influence not only your reactions, but also the reactions of others around you.

They say you can't dig your way out of a deep hole with a shovel. So, if you don't like what life keeps giving you, try to stop doing the same thing over and over expecting a different result. Instead, go within, listen, and observe yourself.

While you notice your perspectives—the lenses through which you view life, yourself, and the world—and the emotions your perspectives generate, be mindful of the actions you take based on all of the above. Notice the consequences these actions produce in your life and in the lives of others.

What do you see when you examine yourself in this way? Do you tend to put yourself or others down, to live in the past, to focus on what's wrong instead of seeing what's good and what's possible? Does your inner critic drive, control, and disempower you? Do you indulge in worry, fear, or regret?

Knowing yourself at this level gives you a new frame of reference and new options. Once you recognize the habitual thoughts and emotions that sabotage you, that produce negative results in your life or lead you in wrong directions, you can begin to accept them and get back on course. It's never too late to learn and evolve. As an old Turkish proverb says, "No matter how far you've gone down the wrong road, turn back."

When you do this work, you begin to discover inner gifts and treasures hidden behind your limitations and imperfections. You realize you are far greater than you knew. You realize that you are capable of extraordinary things you never tried and never imagined you could do.

THE TWO BROADCAST REALMS

Let's deep dive into the two broadcast realms represented on a Broadcast Chart—the Personality Realm and the Soul Realm. To summarize: The Personality Realm is ruled by the conditioned personality, broadcasting hidden subconscious thoughts and beliefs programmed by negative life experiences that generate or perpetuate emotions of fear, anger, and despair.

This realm paints a picture of what you came into this lifetime to master. It is a powerful force to contend with in a physical body in a material world whose broadcasts often garble or drown out the Soul's ethereal voice and wise spiritual counsel. The motto for the Personality Realm is— when you see it, you can transform it.

The Soul Realm is ruled by the Soul, broadcasting higher thoughts and beliefs that generate emotions of peace, trust, and love emanating from your higher Soul perspectives. This realm magnifies your goals for this lifetime. Its broadcasts come from your higher self that transcends the physical reality of life on Earth.

Let's use the analogy of a home stereo system. The bass, the lowest frequency or vibration, is your conditioned personality broadcasts. The treble, the highest frequency or vibration, is your Soul broadcasts. The bass is primal; the treble is melodic.

When the bass anchors the treble, the treble can soar melodically, like a kite on a string. In ideal balance, they work together, complement each other, and incarnate beautiful music. But turn the bass loud enough and it smothers or drowns out the treble and the melody is lost.

How to Soulercise

When your personality broadcasts are your default station, their loud bass programs automatically drown out the melodic voice of your Soul. This limits, and often determines, what you do and don't do, try and don't try, accomplish and fail to accomplish.

But even then, your Soul, your wise and essential self, is still broadcasting its higher thoughts and perspectives, trying to draw your lower mind and personality to its level—to soar melodically.

Having your personality broadcasts as your default station is like being a spiritual "couch potato" who never exercises. If you don't change the channel and develop the mental and emotional muscles of your Soul broadcasts, they weaken and atrophy from lack of use.

But, when you begin to examine all aspects of your personality broadcasts that generate fear, anger, and resentment, you become proficient at noticing your subconscious thoughts and you develop greater self-awareness. As you start to encourage yourself to see your situation from a higher perspective, the more your consciousness expands. You begin to solidify the bridges to the realm of your Soul, and its broadcasts become easier to hear and to follow.

Soulercise guides you to observe and assess the full scope and content of your internal dialogue and how it reflects your personality and Soul broadcasts. Over time, as you practice replacing your conditioned personality thoughts with your Soul's wise, inspiring thoughts, your Soul and its guidance becomes clear and distinct.

As you increasingly exercise the muscles of your Soul and abide in its healing, transformative presence, the more you see yourself, others, and all of the pains and struggles of life from your Soul's perspective. They develop into lessons for enlightenment and fuel for transformation.

As your Soul broadcasts become your natural go-to perspectives, the muscles of your negative personality broadcasts weaken, fade into the background, and lose their power over you. Your subconscious mind gets re-programmed with higher Soul perspectives.

But this only happens when you consistently observe your personality broadcasts during difficult situations and wrestle to change the channel to your Soul's station. Consistency and repetition in this practice strengthens you and makes you fit for life. It is the key to your enlightenment.

Following the *Soulercise* 7 Steps will show you how.

THE 7 STEPS

The diagram titled "The 7 Steps" on the opposite page shows the full content of the *Soulercise* program.

When *Soulercising* in the Personality Realm, the first three steps (1, 2, and 3) and the fourth transitional step (4) are designed to help you recognize and release lower vibrational thoughts and feelings about difficult situations in your life. This unlocks access and builds bridges to your higher vibrational self—your Soul.

When *Soulercising* in the Soul Realm, the last three steps (5, 6, and 7) are designed to replace lower vibrational thoughts and feelings with their higher Soul counterparts and to visualize, affirm, and practice a higher perspective. This allows you to experience your Soul as a tangible, dependable, transforming reality in your daily life.

These 7 Steps are essential tools on the battlefield of life. By following these steps and doing the work, one day and one struggle at a time, you'll begin to live from new Soul perspectives in all of your life circumstances. You'll face difficulties and challenges with

How to Soulercise

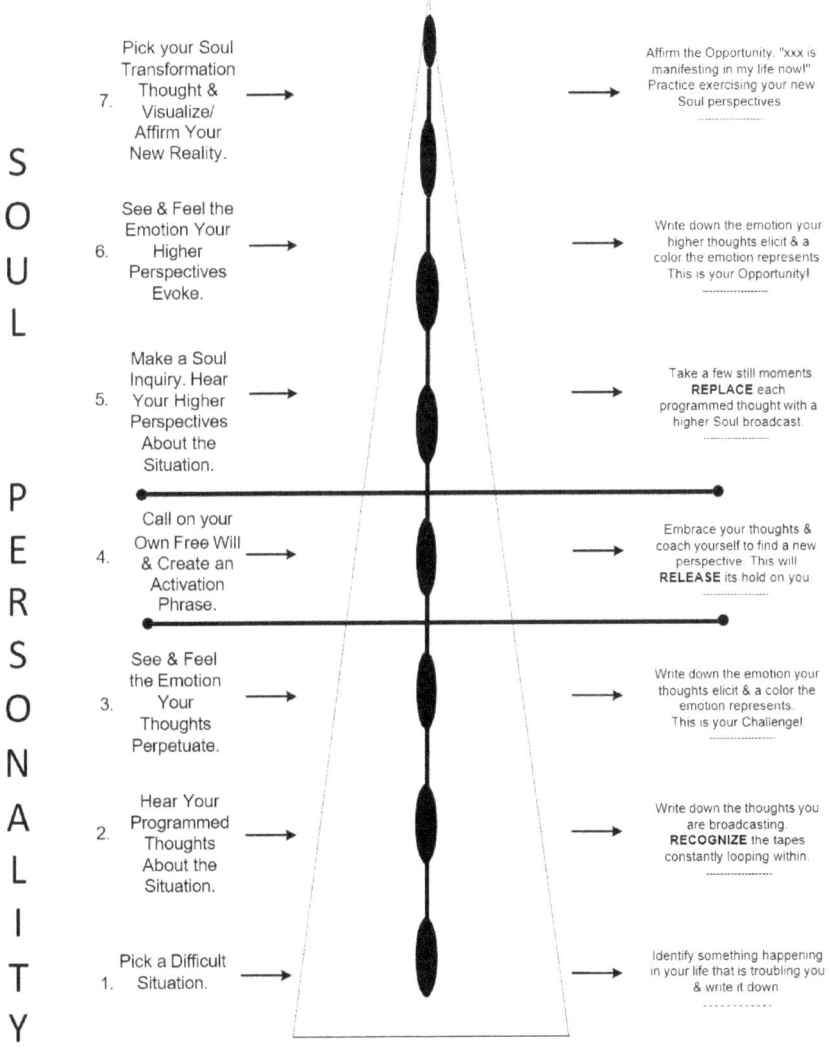

clarity and courage, seeing them as the opportunities they truly are. And if you do the necessary exercise and practice described here, you will grow and evolve over time into a powerful, wise, and loving master of your daily life.

So, when you find yourself in a difficult situation that brings up challenging thoughts and emotions—*Soulercise* it.

To *Soulercise*, build a Broadcast Chart and follow these 7 Steps:

Select a difficult situation in your life. Identify something that is stressful and/or troubling you right now.

Tune into and note the negative personality thoughts you hear. **RECOGNIZE** the broadcasts running in your mind around your situation. They are like a tape recording, constantly looping within.

Choose an emotion from the Challenge column in the Emotion List that your thoughts evoke and/or perpetuate. Choose a color that represents your personality emotion. This is the Challenge you came here to master!

Embrace your lower thoughts and feelings without pushing them away. Love and accept them as they are. This begins to **RELEASE** their hold on you, opening the door to call on your own Free Will and coach yourself to create an Activation Phrase––to spark a new perspective on the situation.

Relax, go within. Tune into and note the higher Soul thoughts you hear. They are always present, like the sun shining behind dark clouds. **REPLACE** each lower personality thought with new perspectives from your higher self.

Choose an emotion from the Opportunity column in the Emotion list that your higher thoughts elicit. Choose a color that represents your new Soul emotion. This is the Opportunity for growth you are seeking!

Visualize yourself responding in a new way and affirm your new Soul thoughts in their completed form. Practice living each day exercising your new perspectives in difficult situations.

EARTHLY CHALLENGES

Soulercise practice is not theoretical or abstract. It always addresses challenging situations, past or present, in your actual life.

When you select a current situation, and track the emotion around it, you'll find that it often leads back to a childhood event. This is because present or recurring challenges and struggles often have their origins in early life situations. Finding the link between such origin events, and current challenges and struggles, can produce meaningful insights and liberating self-awareness.

For example, a challenge I faced growing up was self-criticism and self-doubt, often brought on by my physical appearance. I was born into a wonderful family; to a mom whose fun and loving personality attracted many into our home and to a dad whose box of wise sayings and goal-setting techniques still positively influence me today.

However, I grew up in the Hancock Park/Beverly Hills area of Los Angeles, where models, actors, and actresses set the standards for attractiveness. My body did not match the Hollywood "red carpet" ideal. I inherited a slow metabolism, easily gained weight, and had a fairly large frame.

My parents, who wanted what was best for me, were influenced by the same ideal. So, at age ten, they put me on a diet and exercise program. In grammar school, while other kids brought sandwiches and potato chips for lunch, I brought carrot sticks and a piece of meat with no bread.

To motivate and inspire me, my dad cut out airbrushed magazine pictures of thin, sultry models and pinned them on the bulletin board in my room. At thirteen, they encouraged me to become a "Junior Mannequin" and learn to model. I even did a few fashion shows.

I tried my best to transform myself and become what they wanted me to be. I dieted to lose weight, but I always gained it back. I compared myself to my fellow Junior Mannequins, to magazine models and movie actresses, and to girls in my school who were thinner than me. But no matter how hard I tried, I couldn't live up to the image and meet the expectations.

My parents did what they did with the best intentions. They wanted to help me and increase my chances for success. But the message I deeply internalized was, "I am not thin enough, pretty enough, good enough."

Today, when I see a picture of me at age fifteen, I look beautiful, like I belong on the runway. But at the time, subconsciously, and at times consciously, I felt a deep shame about who I thought I was, and who I thought I wasn't. I felt like a failure in my eyes, and in the eyes of my parents.

In my teens, my negative personality broadcasts reflected and stimulated self-doubt, shame, and insecurity. Every time I looked in the mirror I saw, and heard, "I'm fat."

"I don't look like a model."

"I'll never have a bikini body or be able to wear a bathing suit in public."

For my first date at a high school dance, my mom bought me a special red and white checkered wool pantsuit to wear. I really liked my date, and I was excited and looking forward to the event. But I was a size 12 at age fifteen, and I felt fat and anxious when I put the pantsuit on.

By the time my date came to the door, my negative broadcasts were on full volume. That evening, I was my fun self on the outside, and a shrinking violet on the inside. I felt self-conscious, awkward, and not good enough. The next day, when my date called and just wanted to be friends, my personality broadcast started blaring the "I'm not attractive enough and no one will ever love me" blues.

As an adult, I might not be able to control my slow metabolism. But by *Soulercising*, I can effectively manage my thoughts and emotions, and my reactions.

Now when I diet, I can focus on how healthy I feel rather than how much I weigh. And I can embrace and replace old, conditioned insecurity, embedded since childhood, with genuine confidence. I can't stop disabling thoughts from occurring that trigger this difficult emotion. But I can deal with them forthrightly, courageously, and wisely. I can effectively replace them with Soul thoughts and perspectives that support and empower me.

By choosing which thoughts to entertain, and which ones to let go, I can transform old, conditioned personality thoughts and emotions based in insecurity, abandonment, and fear into Soul thoughts and emotions based in confidence, contentment, and trust.

And the more I choose and contemplate these Soul broadcasts, the more my negative personality broadcasts weaken and fade, the better I feel about myself and my life, and the closer I come to achieving the goals I set for myself before entering this lifetime.

GROWTH, PROGRESS, AND TRANSFORMATION
Difficult challenges and situations not only trigger negative thoughts and intense emotions we came here to work on, but they also often reflect specific life themes.

My early years were a painful struggle with situations that triggered fear and insecurity. But things changed for the better when I realized that I chose my life, and that all of its challenges, situations, and relationships were opportunities to practice trust, develop self-worth, and work to achieve maximum Soul growth. This realization was a transforming shift in perspective, of seeing things not from my personality's point of view, but from my Soul's perspective.

Now I see that incarnating in a family with the theme of accidents, illness, and death motivated me at a young age to pray and reach beyond the visible world for help and understanding. I see that my dad's earnest, loving attempts to motivate and inspire me ultimately served my overall development, my sense of value as a person, and my trust in life.

Most importantly, I see all of the struggles, challenges, and tragedies I've experienced as my curriculum in the school of life. They are landmarks on my path towards a goal we all share and incarnate to achieve—the incremental and increasing perfection of an imperfect self.

Transforming your personality and bringing Soul consciousness into your daily life is a never-ending practice and growth opportunity. There is no end to the progress you can make, the good you can do, and the victories you can achieve. And mistakes, setbacks, and suffering are an unavoidable part of your practice.

You will have good days and bad days, successes and failures.

At times, you may even struggle with negative thoughts and emotions you thought you had previously conquered. But that's okay. You're not doing it wrong. Growth and enlightenment have no straight trajectory. Muscles get stressed and break down before they get stronger. "Three steps forward and two steps back" is a general rule.

Thomas Edison said, "Success is the end result of a series of failures." So, remember, all of the bends, curves, twists, turns, frustrations, and "failures" on your path are essential to your ultimate growth. If you persist in the face of the difficulties and obstacles that life places in your path, you will continue to grow and evolve until you leave this world for the next.

We learn the most about who we are in the face of life's hardships and struggles. We become who we can ultimately be by choosing to exercise our Soul in the face of those hardships and struggles.

In our darkest times, we are never really lost, alone, or forsaken. Our Soul is always in us and with us; always there to support, guide, and teach us. Our Soul, the best friend and ally we will ever have, knows who we really are, where we're going, and why we're here, even when we've forgotten.

So, be patient with yourself. Do your *Soulercise* practice with intention. Appreciate how far you've come instead of despairing over how far you think you have to go. And, as this 12 Step saying reminds us: "Don't quit five minutes before the miracle happens."

Now it's time to *Soulercise!*

CHAPTER 6

Difficult Situations

"A pessimist sees the difficulty in every opportunity. An optimist sees the opportunity in every difficulty."

—Martin Luther King

The first step in the *Soulercise* process is to identify a challenging situation. Then, begin a conscious inquiry into the totality of the situation. This includes your underlying *attitude* – your perspectives, beliefs, thoughts, and feelings about the situation, and about yourself.

Your attitude is an internal force for good or ill that you bring to every moment and every difficulty you face. And it, perhaps more than anything else, is a determining factor in your success or failure to grow through your experience.

Asking Soulful questions—"Who am I?" "Why am I here?" "What is the transformative lesson and potential in this difficult situation?"—plays a major role in attaining Soul consciousness. By doing so, you put a stake in the ground and begin to hold yourself accountable to your life. Then, as you continue and develop your will to learn and grow, you build genuine self-knowledge and healthy, life-positive attitudes that catapult you to change and evolve.

SELF-OBSERVATION AND LIFE REVIEW

You develop self-knowledge through an ongoing practice of self-observation and life review. If you observe your emotions and attitudes over time, you will discover the underlying "programs" that generate them. You will see how these programs—the thoughts about yourself and others you believe to be reality—influence and determine the choices you make, the actions you take or don't take, and the results they produce in your life.

Authentic self-observation increases your chances for inner growth and spiritual success. It is a prerequisite for breaking out of limiting beliefs and mastering the difficult situations you face.

But self-observation is not readily taught or encouraged while growing up, so it's not always easy to achieve unless you make a conscious effort to do so. Taking time to perform a life review—to visualize, as if watching a movie screen, your situation and how you handle it—gives you the opportunity to know where to make adjustments until you are satisfied with what you see during subsequent life reviews.

You will know it's time to practice self-observation and life review by noticing when your buttons get pushed—when something is done or said that results in an immediate and usually emotionally charged reaction. Difficult situations will most often push your buttons, signaling a direct message to take notice and *Soulercise*.

The term "push someone's buttons" first appeared in the United States in the 1920s, when home appliances were invented that merely required the push of a button. Prior to the "home appliance revolution" household chores were difficult and cumbersome. The idea of an immediate response with a simple press of a button gave rise to this saying.

When our "buttons get pushed" it announces loud and clear which thoughts we've programmed and the exact emotion we came here to master. Consider the following example from Betty Bethards: *"If you're very sensitive about your appearance (which could be based upon a fear program: 'I am rejected by others') and someone makes a remark like, 'What a funny looking outfit,' you may feel embarrassed or defensive. Your button just got pushed. But if it weren't a vulnerable spot for you, you'd probably just smile and say, 'Too bad, I like it!'"*

Each time you notice your "buttons getting pushed" and you engage in self-observation and life review, you start to recognize your programs, identify the emotion/weakness you came here to conquer, and develop your spiritual muscles for transformation into a more enlightened existence.

This work is not glamorous. It doesn't make you rich or famous. Self-observation and life review can be difficult and humbling, and it takes practice. But as you do this work, over time you begin take charge of your life, achieve your higher purpose, and crossover with a sense of personal victory.

SOUL MISSION

One thing you can count on in any lifetime is that the universe will provide you with endless opportunities to accomplish what you came here to do, oftentimes in ways you never could have imagined.

On top of the drive for me to obtain a "model's" figure, I grew up being encouraged, even in grammar school, to get good grades so I could go to USC and build a successful career. And I adapted to my parents' wishes. I went to private schools and studied hard, but in the end, I didn't go to USC. Instead, I intuitively followed my Soul mission.

For nearly a decade, my life unfolded through a series of seemingly unrelated adventures, punctuated by setbacks and personal tragedies. I went to college in San Diego and England. I lived on a kibbutz in Israel. I lived with the Huichol Indians and studied yarn painting with a tribal medicine man. I became interested in spirituality and began to meditate.

Next, I attended the Ali Akbar College and studied Indian music. And, with no formal training, I ended up with a lucrative career in the computer industry and also became a neurotechnologist. I married, had my daughter Tamarin (Tam), and lived through both the death of my second husband, Pete, and eventually, the passing of Tam.

Each adventure and tragedy were guided by a higher Soul mission. Each role I took on as a family rebel, a spiritual seeker, a wife, a mother, a widow, and to my family's surprise and mine, a successful businesswoman in the high-tech and neuroscience industry was divinely directed.

Each situation in my life, and its corresponding lessons, changed in time as my Soul fulfilled its higher purpose. I learned through all the twist and turns of my life that my Soul has greater plans than my personality could ever envision. Every setback and tragedy, occupation and achievement, title or status, is part of my Soul plan.

Who I am in reality is greater than anything that happens to my personality; greater than every seemingly wrong turn I take, disappointment I experience, or even goal that I accomplish.

I've had clients who were devasted because they didn't get into the college of their choice, only to call after one semester elated about being at their second-choice college. Or friends who didn't get the job they applied for or the boyfriend/girlfriend they wanted, only to find they eventually were hired at an amazing job or found the relationship of their dreams.

So, amid the challenges and difficulties of this roller coaster life on Earth, strive to see the bigger picture. Even when life delivers devastating blows, remember that you are a divinely created Soul on an eternal journey with a spiritual mission. And you are going to be led to situations and life experiences beyond any role you, your parents, or your teachers consciously had in mind for you. Trust that you will be led to fulfill your true Soul mission.

SETBACKS AND FAILURE
No one wants to fall down or fail, especially when it comes to our careers and our relationships. But at some point, we all do. Failure is an essential and unavoidable part of the learning process that contributes to our ultimate success. When we recognize setbacks and failure as a teacher whose lessons make us wiser and stronger, every setback becomes a steppingstone to our ultimate success.

Remember, life on the Earth plane is a school, difficulties and challenges are our curriculum. They repeat with variations until we learn their lessons, and when we learn these lessons, they either stop repeating or no longer pose a challenge as we grow beyond them.

The workplace is a perfect training ground, providing difficult situations that ensure you accomplish your Soul's objectives. This was especially true for me with the advent of the computer age.

Between 1987 and 2012, I focused on building my career. I

worked for several multi-million dollar technology companies, released numerous "leading-edge" software products, and received prestigious awards and large bonuses beyond my wildest dreams. I managed multiple software QA teams and often felt like a champion on top of the world!

Also, during that same time, downsizing was a common business strategy as senior management was often under pressure from stockholders to not just produce good profits but extraordinary profits—cutting employment costs was the easiest solution.

As a result, not only did several companies that I worked for downsize and announce layoffs, but also thousands of dollars in my stock options became worthless overnight. My financial security often vanished like a puff of smoke on a windy day. In a short time, I'd go from "the thrill of victory" to "the agony of defeat."

By 2001, I was an experienced veteran, but during post-layoff job searches, most companies were hiring younger engineers with computer science degrees for lower salaries and less equity. My future often seemed precarious, and my personality broadcasted programs generating fear and anxiety. Common themes were: "I'll never find another job with the same investment opportunities," and "I have to lower my expectations and take whatever I can get to survive."

When I was much younger, I believed my personality broadcasts. When things were going my way, I thought I was invincible. And when life scattered my fortune to the winds, I thought my life was ruined. Eventually, I became more skilled at not succumbing to my personality's prophecies of doom, at focusing on learning the lessons embedded in these career crash-and-burn experiences, and on making the most out of this "opportunity for growth."

Soul Bridges

I used my spiritual tools to process my personality's negative thoughts and feelings and let my Soul show me the way forward—affirming, visualizing, and holding Soul consciousness. I took practical actions to move forward where I could, and as it turned out, instead of needing a Ph.D., "equivalent years of industry experience" was my golden ticket to securing a new job.

In 2004, EMC, an enterprise data storage company based in Massachusetts, had just acquired VMware, a Silicon Valley virtual machine company, and now wanted to expand into the SMB (small and mid-sized business) market. So, around that same time they acquired Dantz Development Corp., the makers of a backup software program I was managing at the time.

It was a successful acquisition, but after three years of hard work and dedication, executives from both EMC and VMware arrived at Dantz unannounced with the news of a downsize. This time, I, along with several of my team, a few hand-picked engineers, and most of sales and marketing were saved and moving to a new VMware office located in San Francisco. The rest of Dantz's employees were laid off.

Then, on August 14, 2007, after only a few months at my new job, the miracle happened—VMware went public! We all gathered at corporate headquarters to watch the Wall Street "sounding of the bell." In a moment, my stock options finally became a windfall! After nearly 30 years in the computer industry and multiple seeming failures, I sold my stock and started my own company—NeuroFit®, a NeuroFitness Training Center to "Cross-Train Your Brain".

But more important than these financial benefits were the lessons I learned from those difficult years. I learned that losing what I had wasn't the real catastrophe. The real catastrophe was when I let external events dominate and define me. It was being so focused on material outcomes and on worldly ideas of winning and losing, success and failure, that I forgot my higher purpose.

Most importantly, I learned firsthand that the greatest victory was persevering in good faith through all the "ups and downs," recognizing when my "buttons got pushed," performing life reviews, and engaging in consistent self-observation while striving to learn the lessons imparted through both failure and success. For every "failure" and setback contains lessons that, once learned, become spiritual victories that empower you to even greater realms of success.

HIGHER PURPOSE

At some point, we all find ourselves in situations we think we can't handle. While our conditioned personality would never volunteer for such experiences, our Soul did exactly that, and for a higher purpose—to master life's difficult situations and evolve into higher states of being.

To manage your finances, you must know your income and your expenses, create a budget, set financial goals, and more. To control your diet, you must know what food is good or bad for you, how much you need to eat, how to deal with unhealthy cravings, and more. To achieve Soul growth, you must know the kind of thoughts you tend to think and emotions you tend to feel. You need to know the stress triggers and circumstances that activate negative, self-sabotaging patterns when challenged and how to transform them.

All negative, disempowering thoughts, feelings, and the behaviors they trigger in you have a purpose—they force you to seek change. They compel you to notice how you think about, talk to, and treat yourself and others; how you criticize and judge yourself and others; how your disempowering default personality patterns produce negative effects in your life, while you imagine that life was working against you or doing it to you.

When you explore the totality of a difficult situation, you begin to notice that you are the one who enters into, and often co-creates, unhealthy situations that cause you stress. You are the one who entertains the negative thoughts, emotions, and perspectives that disempower you, make you suffer, and needlessly complicate your life.

As a simple example, the weather may be hot, humid, and unbearable, generating feelings of discontentment and frustration. But at any moment, you can change your perspective and think of this same day as filled with sunny skies, green hills, and a beautiful sunset, filling you with appreciation and contentment. This simple mind shift can be done at any moment, for any situation in your daily life.

With this knowledge, you can begin to make your thoughts and emotions work for you instead of against you. You can't control the people, situations, and relationships in your life, but you can control how you react to them. If you use the things that happen to you and around you to learn about yourself, others, and life, you will grow stronger, deeper, and wiser. You will begin to master yourself and your daily life.

It can be difficult to access a particular emotion until something ignites that emotion within you. That's okay. You don't need (nor is it possible) to *Soulercise* all of your challenging emotions at once. Simply observe and track each emotion as it occurs. And remember, all difficulties and challenges reflect key life themes you chose to work on before you incarnated. And when you know the key themes that define your life struggles, you've unveiled their higher purpose.

The 7 Steps in the *Soulercise* process will help you to accomplish this.

When you take the first step and pick a difficult situation to work with, you begin the process of getting in touch with the higher purpose the situation provides, and you start the process of building bridges––shifting from your conditioned personality's point of view to your Soul's perspective. Your personality may find the situation frustrating, painful, or even tragic. Your Soul knows the higher purpose and sees it as a lesson and an amazing opportunity to gain self-mastery.

If the primary purpose of your journey in this Earth school is to get to know yourself—to hear what you think and see how you react and why, then the goal is to graduate with honors. Profound inner resources for learning, growth, wisdom, and transformation exist within you, and they become extremely available under difficult circumstances, perhaps like your present situation. So, let's start digging!

STEP 1: Pick A Situation—Identify Something Stressful
In this chapter you will follow Step 1 only. So, pick a difficult, stressful, or traumatic situation in your life and start building a Broadcast Chart to map out your situation. To do this:

1. Copy the chart on the next page, download it from the website www.CindyReynolds.com, or create a chart of your own on a piece of paper or in a journal. A Broadcast Chart contains seven thought wave lines (four wavy and three straight lines) in the bottom half—the Personality

Soul Bridges

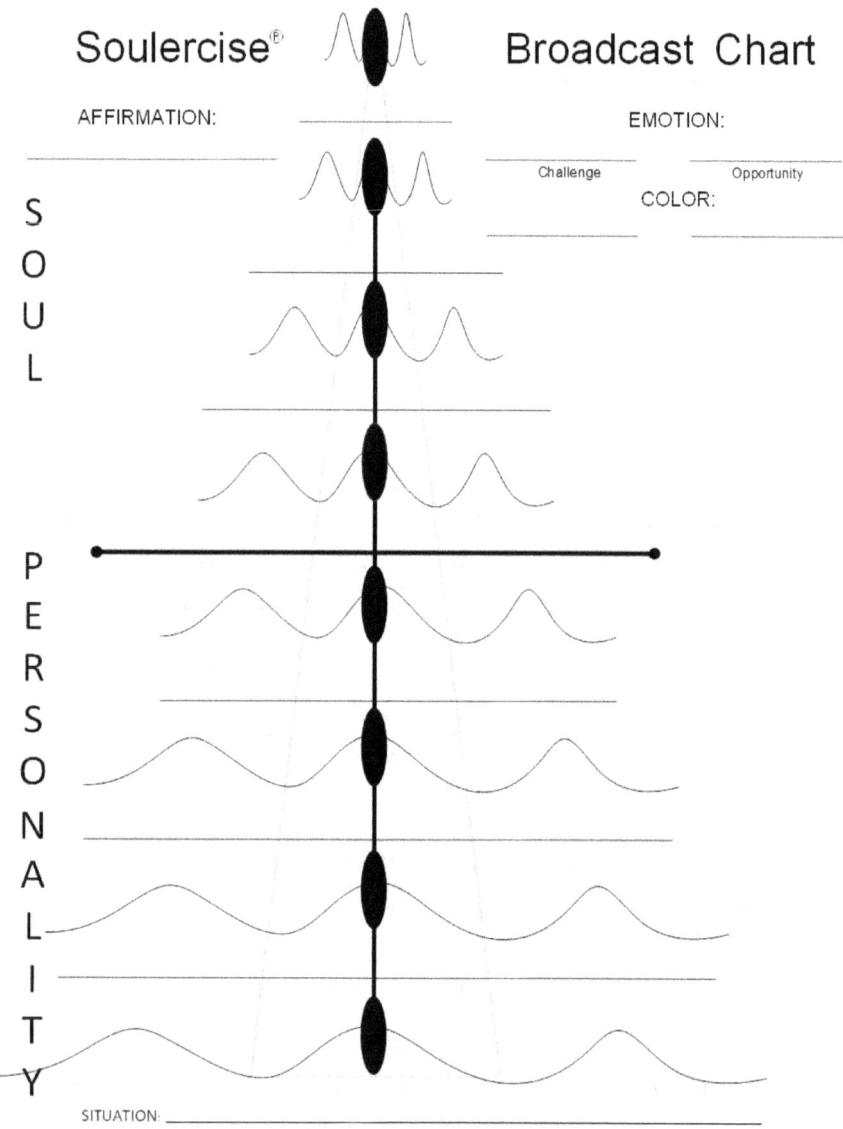

Realm—and seven thought wave lines (four wavy and three straight) on the upper half— the Soul Realm.

2. To begin, write down the situation you picked next to the word "Situation" at the bottom of the chart. For example, "I didn't get the perfect job I interviewed for."

As you continue and learn about each Step in subsequent chapters, this sample situation—"I didn't get the perfect job I interviewed for"—will be used as an example for how to work the 7 Steps and fill out your personal Broadcast Chart. It will be designated as the "Dream Job" example or scenario.

Also, as you get more proficient in using the Steps, you don't have to build a physical Broadcast Chart for every situation. But the time and effort you put into it will correspond to the benefits you get out of it.

So, it's good to fill out full written Broadcast Charts while reading the following chapters and during subsequent difficult situations until you really understand the steps and the process. After that, a mental chart can be as effective as a written one. This will help you *Soulercise* when you're at work, at school, or even driving in your car, and integrate Soul consciousness into your daily life.

CHAPTER 7
Personality Thoughts & Emotions

"Opportunity is missed by most people because it is dressed in overalls and looks like work."
—Thomas Edison

Consider that since the Earth plane is a school—that you chose to come here to learn from your experiences and master your thoughts and emotions—then if you fulfill your Soul plan and accomplish your goals to your Soul's satisfaction, you won't have to reincarnate in a physical body and do it again!

For centuries, spiritual teachers have explained the concept of reincarnation and how it takes a Soul more than one lifetime and many different situations to learn all of its lessons and vibrationally evolve into higher realms. The next two Soulercise Steps covered in this chapter provide more tools towards this goal.

VIBRATIONAL REALITY
We humans emanate the energy vibrations of our thoughts and emotions from birth to death, and from lifetime to lifetime. Since most of these emanations come from our conditioned personality rather

than our Soul, this negative, self-reinforcing loop of perceptions, thoughts, and feelings is a web of illusion we weave and experience as our subjective reality from one incarnation to the next.

In fact, this is one way that we create our own reality. And it is what Buddhism calls Samsara.

When we believe our looping thoughts and emotions, we embrace a low-vibrational reality and are born into that same reality lifetime after lifetime. And when we act based on these illusions, we create perpetual desires, chaos, and stress in our life. This is how, according to some spiritual traditions, we become locked in a cycle of death and rebirth.

But by observing our low-vibration complex of thoughts and feelings, we can transcend and gain mastery over them. We can embrace a high-vibrational reality and eventually achieve the ultimate in higher levels of Soul consciousness.

As personalities, yes, we make mistakes. We become angry, sad, fearful, and at times, overwhelmed. We maintain stressful thoughts and feelings, that by themselves are not a problem. But they become a problem when we believe them to be our only reality and lock ourselves into lower vibrational states of being.

Think of the personality as a clunky 4-cylinder car. It gets you around, but it is unreliable. It lacks power, wastes fuel, and it discharges toxic emissions into the atmosphere. It emanates negativity with low-vibrational thoughts and emotions that keep you trapped in the illusion that this is your only reality.

Now, think of the Soul as a powerful 12-cylinder dream car. It is sturdy, reliable, and fuel efficient. It is built to last forever and will take you wherever you want to go. And it emanates another reality of high-vibrational thoughts and emotions that uplift, motivate, and transform you and often those around you.

So, how do you upgrade your clunky personality vehicle to a deluxe Soul craft while mastering your daily life? You assemble your *Soulercise* Broadcast Chart.

Putting the pieces of your chart together teaches you how to build bridges beyond the single-point perspectives you currently experience. It is a tool to discern the higher perspectives, thoughts, and emotions of your Soul mingling amongst those of your personality. It is a means by which you can practice self-observation and learn to catch and release negative personality thoughts in the moment and replace them with uplifting and clarifying Soul perspectives.

Over time, this leads you to sustain the high-vibrational states of Soul consciousness, both in this lifetime and the next.

In *Soulercise* Step 2 you will practice hearing and recognizing your lower personality thoughts, or broadcasts. In Step 3 you will identify the emotion these thoughts trigger and see how it overrides your rational mind, causing you to react to situations in a way that produces the results you experience in your life now.

Both of these steps guide you to recognize, and to view with understanding, and even humor, your negative personality thoughts and the unpleasant feelings they generate.

Your negative, low-vibrational thoughts are often single-point perspectives that fall into four general categories:

Your self-worth:
"I'm not good enough."
"I'll never get into a good college."
"I fail at everything."
"He/she would never be interested in me."
"I can't please everyone."

Your body or your looks:
"I'm too fat."
"I'm ugly."
"My nose is too big."
"I'm over the hill."

Other people:
"My boss is a jerk and he has it in for me."
"My co-workers are idiots."
"My mother always judges me."
"My spouse is unsupportive."
"People don't appreciate me."
"My father doesn't believe in me."
"My kids will never get it."

Your core negative beliefs about life:
"There's no justice."
"No matter how good you are, it still comes down to luck."
"People don't care."
"Life is unfair."
"Things don't work out."

Do any of these sound familiar to you? As you go deeper within, observing your thoughts in the light of these four categories, you begin to recognize the negative thoughts your personality has been broadcasting for years, not quietly but with hypnotic power. And you start to see how you take these thoughts for granted, objectively believing them to be the only truth.

By assembling *Soulercise* Broadcast Charts, you begin to realize that within these thoughts are underlying patterns and themes that form the internal architecture of your personality-bound life.

You start to see how the internal structure of negative beliefs and single-point perspectives reflects a core lack of faith in yourself, in others, and in life.

This structure mediates and skews your perceptions of, and your relationship to, every situation and challenge you face, often producing the very results you fear and try to avoid.

Remember, thoughts are things. And this low-vibrational reality will continue to operate in this way until you see and understand it in the light of Soul consciousness and do the work to transform and grow beyond it.

The bottom line is, don't only believe everything you automatically think! You are actually much more than your conditioned personality leads you to believe. By observing yourself and then looking beyond for higher perspectives, you can release the painful illusions of your conditioned personality and learn to maintain the high-vibrational reality of your Soul.

HEAR YOUR PERSONALITY THOUGHTS

Most of us believe our negative personality broadcasts as if they were news delivered by a trusted news anchor. We rarely question the reality of the broadcast, the perspective of the anchor, or the internal structure they represent. So, let's do that now.

What do you hear when you listen to your personality thoughts? Are your broadcasts telling you that you're a failure? That your parent doesn't care about you and rejects you? That no one respects you or accepts you for who you are? Or that life is unfair and you'll never be able to fulfill your dreams?

Failure to hear your personality thoughts, to challenge and look beyond such broadcasts, tacitly validates their negative, self-sabotaging message. Yet many of us allow these negative, disempowering thoughts to drone on unchallenged, in the background of our minds, for years.

To understand the effects that this might have on you and produce in your life, re-read the four categories of broadcast messages in the previous section. Notice that each message communicates an absolute negative idea. Notice that each idea seems designed to make you feel disheartened, powerless, even hopeless—that your cup is half-empty. Notice the core lack of faith in yourself, others, and life embedded in each idea.

Now consider: How do you think you would feel and live, and what kind of life do you think you would create, based on these ideas? Can you see how you might stop trying to do your best in the face of adversity? Can you see how you might become resigned to the way things are? Can you see how such negative ideas broadcasting in the background of your mind for years might become self-fulfilling prophecies?

Now, re-read the messages again with a critical eye and ask yourself: *Are they literally the only perspectives?*

A famous study conducted in a San Francisco elementary school by Harvard professor Robert Rosenthal showed how projecting beliefs and expectations onto others can affect their behavior and performance. Rosenthal randomly selected a small group of students in each class and told their teachers they had high IQs. He told the teachers that the rest of the students were average.

Over the next two years, Rosenthal monitored teacher/student interactions and student performance levels. He noted that the teachers treated the high IQ students as special and treated the rest as ordinary. Not surprisingly, the students perceived and treated as special significantly outperformed those perceived and treated as average.

The study concluded that the students unconsciously adapted to, and performed at the level of, the beliefs and expectations their teachers communicated to them through countless verbal and non-verbal cues. Other similar studies have reached similar conclusions.

Just like a child's sense of themselves is largely formed in response to positive and negative feedback they receive from those they depend on, if you tell yourself, and come to believe, that you are bad, stupid, incompetent, or worthless, you will tend to see and treat yourself that way and feed your feelings of insecurity, anger, or worry. You will unconsciously adapt to, and perform at, the level of those programmed beliefs.

If you believe that others are bad, stupid, and incompetent, not worthy of your trust and good will, you will overtly or subtly treat them that way. They will sense this, consciously or subconsciously, and respond in a way that confirms your negative beliefs and projections. This will negatively impact your relationships. You will feel increasingly separate from others. And you will suffer.

The solution to this life of stressful illusions is to stop and hear your personality thoughts as they arise. Listen to what you are saying to yourself and realize that your perspective affects everything that happens to you. A continuous practice of hearing your lower personality thoughts, and a simple change in your mindset, gives you the opportunity to transform your emotions into your Soul's wisdom perspective.

SEE REACTIVE EMOTIONS
As a rule, do you feel jealous, insecure, abandoned, criticized, or shamed? Do you feel that life has cheated you, that your body has failed you, that your parents, siblings, kids, or spouse don't

appreciate you, or that your friends are mean to you or your boss and co-workers don't like you and disrespect you?

While observing your challenging emotions with the help of your *Soulercise* Broadcast Chart, you will discover that many, or perhaps most of them, are generated and/or perpetuated by one-point perspectives on situations in your life.

As you learn to recognize, release, and replace these limited perspectives with healthy empowering, energizing thoughts and feelings that reflect new perspectives—your Soul's perspectives—you will begin to generate feelings of trust and love for who you *really* are. And you will increasingly awaken from the lonely, limiting destiny this single-point perspective has imposed on you.

And remember, the negative feelings your personality broadcasts generate are important. They are the voice of your conscience telling you where your attitude and behavior are out of alignment with your Soul. They are signposts telling you to examine yourself with painstaking honesty.

Acknowledge and accept difficult feelings. Real acceptance is not passive resignation. It is a rigorously honest self-assessment without self-defeating judgments and brutal condemnation. Accepting the painful feelings you have previously been unable or unwilling to acknowledge is courageous, humbling, and transformative.

It isn't wrong to have negative feelings. But it is confusing and agonizing to believe them, and harmful or destructive to act them out. You cannot stop them by an act of will. You can't get rid of them by fighting them, or by feeling bad and guilty. But you *can* recognize them.

You can see their purpose and value for your growth in self-knowledge and wisdom. You can practice with them. You can observe and learn from them. And then, you can release and replace them with inspiring and energizing Soul thoughts that generate healthy feelings and reactions.

Most importantly, this is not just a mental process. Our emotions must be fully acknowledged before we can grow beyond them. We all unconsciously repress painful emotions that we don't feel strong enough to face. But you cannot embrace, release, or transform emotions you have repressed or even medicated away for years. In this process, all of the reactive and painful emotions you pressed down into the unconscious need to be seen and embraced.

Let's say you are at a family gathering. You are feeling strong and confident. Then a sibling says something hurtful. Your buttons get pushed. You feel vulnerable and your self-esteem plummets. You want to leave the gathering and nurse your wound.

Instead, you *Soulercise* in the moment. You identify the difficult situation. You recognize the automatic looping personality thoughts the situation has triggered. You consciously observe your emotional reaction to the situation. What emotion is it? This is the Challenge you came here to master!

Now a painful incident that made you feel like a hapless victim becomes an opportunity for growth in Soul Consciousness.

TAKE SUPPORTIVE ACTIONS

Yet sometimes emotions come up that are still too intense for you. So be gentle. Don't push yourself too hard. Remember, slow and steady wins the race.

You develop emotional strength the same way that you develop physical strength. You don't try to bench press 300 pounds in your first week in the gym. You start where you are and make incremental progress over time. And if you exercise consistently, gradually increasing the weight as your strength increases over time, you may eventually bench press 300 pounds.

When turbulent thoughts and emotions are given free reign, they can overwhelm and imprison you in hellish states that Buddhism calls lower *bardos*. *Soulercising* disturbing thoughts and emotions that arise is important, but sometimes you may also need to take supportive actions to find relief.

When you develop a comprehensive *Soulercise* program, it can be helpful to pair it with practices that release stress, bring you into balance, and restore clarity and perspective.

It's also good if you can directly resolve your issues with others through meaningful dialogue. Perhaps you can discuss difficulties with a spouse, family member, friend, pastor, or therapist. Sometimes it helps to lovingly confront a person who has hurt you and let them know how their actions have affected you.

If this is not an option, you can achieve positive results using various forms of exercise, meditation, or neurotechnology such as neurofeedback and neurostimulation to rebalance dysregulated brainwave patterns that have you locked into fear, anxiety, or depression.

Spending time in nature also helps to calm your mind and emotions, release stress, and regain a healthy perspective.

In summary, difficult emotions contain vital information and energy long repressed in the unconscious. We access the information and energy trapped in our repressed emotions by facing them directly. And, as we learn our lessons and meet our challenges head-on, we can wrestle with them to the point of mastery.

Jacob in the Old Testament wrestled all night (the time of darkness) with an angel. And he refused to let go until dawn came (the time of new light). Then the angel gave him a divine gift and departed. In the same way, our challenges are our struggle in the darkness. When we persist and refuse to give up, new light comes, and we are given the gift of mastery.

By meeting and wrestling with our challenges face to face, we develop the willpower, emotional strength, self-knowledge, and other essential qualities needed to fulfill our potential and move on into higher vibrational realms. And that is the point, after all.

So, let's continue.

STEP 2: Note Your Thoughts—Hear Your Looping Tapes
In Chapter 6, you chose a situation in your life where you are experiencing a difficulty, challenge, or dilemma. Now you will work within the Personality Realm. Here you will tune into and write down your personality thoughts in the lower half of your chart—the Personality Realm, or you can simply turn your attention inward and focus with awareness on these thoughts as they arise.

1. Beginning at the bottom, on first straight line (line #1) of the Broadcast Chart you started in Chapter 6, contemplate your situation and write down the first thought that comes. For example, in the "Dream Job" scenario, if you didn't get hired for a job you really wanted, you might write, "Nothing ever works out for me."

2. Write down successive thoughts that come to you—the programs you broadcast—around your own personal situation, or at least make mental notes of them. Do this until you have filled in each of the straight lines #1 – #3 in the Personality Realm, or mentally noted three thoughts. (Do not fill in the thick black line #4. This line is a transition line reserved for a later part of the *Soulercise* process.)

For example, in the "Dream Job" scenario you may hear and note angry thoughts or self-critical hopeless thoughts: "Those jerks, they don't have a clue what they are doing!"

Or "Who would ever want to hire me?"

But no matter what thoughts come, simply RECOGNIZE them, don't censor them or try to find better thoughts instead. Just contemplate your situation and write down or mentally note all the thoughts you hear.

3. Now, take a moment to read again the thoughts you wrote down in the Personality Realm of your Broadcast Chart, or to reflect on the thoughts you mentally noted. Does this chart fully reflect the thoughts you tend to tell yourself in response to your situation? Be sure that it does before you continue. If you need to write more, do so on the wavy lines, or on the back of the page.

If you find yourself writing variations of previous thoughts you've already written down, you are probably complete.

If you find it difficult to get in touch with your thoughts, look at the four categories mentioned earlier. Consider each category deeply, until you see the negative personality thoughts, and the core beliefs they contain, that have been driving you, limiting you, and causing you uncertainty, anxiety, or pain.

In reality, your thoughts are just information and energy passing through the angelic Soul you truly are, whose nature is pure spirit. Your challenging situations, and the thoughts and emotions they stir up, show you where you are weak or strong, clear or confused, prepared or unprepared, developed or undeveloped. They call you to new growth. And to grow to your next level in any area, you must wrestle with problems and challenges beyond your present capacity.

It helps to see all the negative thoughts that pass through you as temporary ripples from a stone tossed into a vast lake, whose water is spirit. Know that you are the water and not the ripples passing across the surface. The more you can accept, and see in this way, the thoughts that have you in their grip, the freer you become in relation to them, and the freer you become in life.

STEP 3: Identify a Lower Emotion—Meet Your Challenge!

1. Turn to the Emotion List in Chapter 4. Choose one from the "Challenge" column that represents the emotion your thoughts evoke. Which emotion is most intense for you right now? This is one of the challenges you came here to master. In the "Dream Job" example, the emotion with the most charge, or intensity, might be "Fear" relative to not getting hired for the perfect job and needing money to survive.

    Note: Only work with one emotion at a time. If more than one emotion or feeling arises relative to your situation, work with the one that has the greatest charge. And if you experience emotions that are not on the list, you can add them to the list.

2. On the top of your Broadcast Chart under the word "Emotion" write down the "Challenge" emotion you picked—"Fear" in this example. What color does the feeling of Fear represent? Write down the color. For the "Dream Job" example the color would be "Red."

3. Now, take a moment to feel your reactive emotion swirling within you. See this emotion without judgment, without

resistance, as energy sensations, which it also is. Where does it live? In your chest? Your throat? Your stomach? Sometimes a powerful emotion feels like a high-voltage electric current or has a burning sensation. Some emotions feel like gentle currents of flowing or vibrating energy.

Sometimes feelings are too painful to reflect upon. That's okay. Feel instead the color that you chose. What feeling does that color generate inside of you? See your emotion as an energy state. And observe the ebb and flow, the passing and changing of the feeling as it comes and goes.

Steps 2 and 3 are an important part of *Soulercising*. As you recognize your thoughts and write them down (or mentally note them) on your Broadcast Chart, and identify the emotion swirling within, you begin to recognize and understand your challenge for what it is—a living process within you.

You can't stop hardships from happening. But if you use them to consistently engage in the *Soulercise* process during challenging situations, you will deepen your self-awareness, strengthen your will, and hone your spiritual intuition. You will learn vital lessons from your most difficult experiences and discover the meaning and value of your suffering.

Your spiritual center of gravity will gradually shift and you'll become aware of things you never thought you would, and never could, as simply a personality struggling to survive in the material world. Most importantly, you set wheels in motion that move you forward on your path into new dimensions of being.

CHAPTER 8

The Turning Point

*"The highest form of human intelligence
is to observe yourself without judgement."*

—J. Krishnamurti

Congratulations—you've arrived at a *Soulercise* turning point! Changing the channel begins here, in Step 4, with a free will choice to consciously embrace your thoughts and feelings as a vital part of who you are, and to stop the train of negative thoughts by activating positive change. It's not always easy to activate change, but it's worth the struggle and effort. The more you practice, the easier it becomes to conquer all of the challenges of daily life.

If you've followed your *Soulercise* program to this point, you've completed the Personality Realm in your Broadcast Chart around a challenging situation. You've recognized the lower personality thoughts this event stimulated. And you've identified your primary emotional response to your situation. So here you stand at the turning point between living a life riddled with fear, insecurity, and resentment, or a life guided by trust, confidence, and forgiveness.

Will you continue to let your lower personality thoughts and emotions create needless stress, conflicted relationships, and avoidable crises in your life? Or will you call upon the will to embrace your emotions and change the channel from these discouraging, counterproductive broadcasts to your Soul's higher, enlightening perspectives?

Choosing to embrace and release your thoughts and the emotion they invoke prepares you for Step 5 and 6, where you can perceive your situation from a higher Soul perspective. But every opportunity is an unfulfilled possibility until it is seized with a will and used with purposeful intention. When you activate the will and intention to embrace who you are and do the work to activate a change in your perspective, a new way of living and being in the world gradually opens up to you.

FAITH AND FREE WILL

Whichever road in life we choose, we can always find comfort in the fact that we are watched over and helped by higher beings in unseen dimensions. They are as real as we are, far more wise and powerful, and their guidance, blessings, and light are available to us here in the material world. But they cannot intervene in our lives without our free will consent.

Remember, we sat with these same beings before we entered the Earth plane. In addition to planning with us the events, crises, challenges, and setbacks which would strengthen our spirit and even contribute to the good of mankind, they also remain accessible to us while we are here. We may not see them, but they are there, waiting to be called upon in any moment of need. And whether we turn and call on them or not is up to us.

We access these and other extra-dimensional resources through two spiritual faculties—faith and free will—the same faculties we employ to live a more enlightened life.

Free will is the power we have to choose, consent, act, and create in a conscious and deliberate manner rather than by impulse or instinct. Our instincts guide and preserve us to a degree. But our free will allows us to activate meaningful changes and catalyze new developments in our lives. It is what drives us to call on a higher power and to search for higher perspectives in the difficult challenges we are faced with during our time on Earth.

Real faith, on the other hand, is not wishful thinking, childish belief in fantasies, or a mere coping mechanism. It is the intuitive, life-changing acceptance of a transcendent reality whose divine light, power, and love sustains us in each moment of our existence.

Faith relieves much of the stress, anxiety, and doubt we experience in a material world defined by uncertainty, suffering, and impermanence. It helps us persevere in the face of adversity and to be deepened and matured, rather than defeated or destroyed, by our struggles.

Faith and free will must walk together, hand in hand. Neither can do what the other does. Faith counterbalances and empowers our free will, but never replaces it. However great our faith, we must still grapple with and resolve the problems and tests of daily life that we agreed to before entering this world.

My own need for faith and free will evolved exponentially while raising a daughter whose contributory purpose (sharing in the cause of something for the greater good) was fostered by severe physical fallibilities.

While pregnant and preparing Tamarin's "Earth suit" inside my belly, I continually prayed to give birth to a Soul who would grow up and help others. Little did I know how true it is that you need to be specific in what you ask for and, as it is often said, answers to prayers come in unexpected ways.

Tamarin's contributory purpose developed at a young age and progressed throughout her life, continually driving us to call on faith and free will to search for deeper meanings.

In a preschool accident Tam sustained her first concussion, and then suffered subsequent concussions from a car and a snowboarding accident. These injuries left her fallible and in need of medical attention as a young adult.

As a Type 1 diabetic, Tamarin experienced a devastating series of medical challenges and multiple life-threatening illnesses which required lengthy hospitalizations over many years, caused immense physical and emotional suffering, and included a malignant fifteen-pound tumor that eventually took her life at forty-two years old.

During times of trouble, I wondered if her Soul Plan had gone off the rails and consulted medium channel Leanne Rosko Doty. She told me that Tamarin wanted to take the bull by the horns in this lifetime, and before either of us incarnated, Tam had asked me if I was up for the challenges posed by the chronic medical problems that were a key part of her Soul plan. According to Leanne, my reply to Tamarin was essentially, "Heck yes, let's do it!"

This doesn't seem rational to my human personality that I would take on such a journey. But again, it makes total sense from my Soul's perspective.

What rational human being would choose to undergo such challenges, let alone be able to endure them? Yet many Souls choose paths of great adversity that offer maximum growth potential and Soul transformation or that contribute to the greater good—to the evolution of a particular field on Earth. My faith in these truths and my will to switch from my fears and maintain this higher perspective was an ongoing and life-changing practice.

Tamarin's Soul Chart, with its numerous setbacks, debilitating medical crises, and near-death events would be difficult for anyone to bear. But the strength and fortitude that made her a rhythmic gymnast on the USA National Team got her through every challenge and catastrophe. Many times, giving up and throwing in the towel seemed like a reasonable option, but she never did.

When medical situations became critical, I would call on my faith and free will. I'd remind myself that Tam chose her path, and I chose to be her ally and support team in sickness and health, from beginning to end. We shared a Soul commitment to a common mission: Face every crisis head-on. Learn the lessons and achieve maximum growth from whatever life brings us. And help others however we can along the way.

In the depths of these crises, we both asked in faith for help from above and called on our own free will to switch to a higher perspective. We worked to accept the situations we could not change and re-committed to the plan we shared.

During the most difficult times, we offered each other a comforting shoulder to lean on. When things seemed hopeless, faith was our foundation. And it was enough to get us through. But our faith wasn't given. We chose it with a will in the face of adversity, day after day, year after year. And as our faith and our will grew stronger and deeper, so did we.

Once Tam accomplished all that she came here to do, and the time came for her to transition from this Earth, it was her body that gave out, not her will. Tamarin's last words before crossing over were, "There's a temple in the sky and everything is reverberating!"

The Turning Point

It was my faith that allowed me to understand she had gone to a good place and my will to find peace that helped to offset my grief.

Most importantly, Tamarin's contributory purpose is still going strong. Her Soul *is* still helping others—family, friends, clients, and even medical professionals. Tam's complicated medical crises initiated research, doctor collaboration, and retrospective knowledge that will help future patients. Many family and friends have told me, "When my life seems tough, I think of Tam and realize I have nothing to complain about."

Or, "Watching Tam reminded me how to remain strong amongst adversity."

But most often I hear, "If she could manage her difficulties, I can get through mine."

Even the mortician said, "When anyone complains to me about their life, all I have to do is show them this death certificate with all the critical illnesses she endured."

Tamarin's medical challenges, paired with the evolution of computer technology and advancements in the field of neuroscience, also profoundly altered my professional career track. Tam's concussions and mTBI diagnosis led us to EEG Biofeedback (Neurofeedback), NeuroModulation, and other NeuroTechnologies as an alternative form of treatment for head injury without medication.

I began to research and study these new technologies, to learn how they worked and what they could do. I traveled all over the country and interviewed leaders in the field and settled on a program that significantly helped Tamarin. And as a direct result of Tam's challenges, NeuroFit is still fulfilling her contributory purpose and is still today profoundly helping others.

If hardship and calamity are the dark side of life, opportunity and growth are the light in that darkness, foretelling the coming dawn.

So, when adversity comes, work to muster faith and free will, knowing that prayers *are* answered and faith-fueled free will is a spiritual force that can move mountains over time. The 7 *Soulercise* Steps gave us the tools to do this, to develop self-mastery and wisdom out of the hardships and tragedies of life. And they can do the same for you.

CONSCIOUS CHOICE

You've probably heard that "You become what you meditate on," and, "You bind yourself to that which you oppose."

But did you know that *any* habitual focus and perspective constitutes your primary meditation in life? If you meditate on joy for an hour a day, but spend 12 hours a day anxiously focusing on your problems, what is your primary meditation and what will it produce? Simple math will give you the answer. The habitual focus on problems drowns out joy and elevates anxiety, blinding you to expanded Soul perspectives that contain the solutions to your problems.

When the conditioned personality myopically focuses on and magnifies problems—rather than seeking solutions from a place of wisdom—this is a default choice, not a conscious choice. So, in Step 4, you make the conscious choice to shift from an unconscious struggle with your emotion to conscious action you intentionally aspire to take.

Here, at the turning point in your *Soulercise* program, you first pause for a moment to consciously call on your free will to accept and embrace your current thoughts and overriding emotion.

Real acceptance is not passive resignation. It is an active and honest self-assessment without judgement that is courageous, humbling, and transformative. Making the conscious choice to embrace your emotion releases its hold on you and opens the doorway to seeing new perspectives and responding differently.

Then you call on your free will once again and summon the motivation to handle your situation wisely. This provides a platform from which you can coach yourself to activate a shift in your attention from the personality's negative thoughts and emotions about the issue to liberating Soul perspectives.

Just as you coach and motivate yourself to run further and longer when training for a marathon, or work harder and longer when building a career, by sheer will power, the turning point comes as you embrace who you are and motivate yourself to shift, *on any issue*, from a personality focus that generates fear, shame, or insecurity, to expanded Soul perspectives.

Once you've made this conscious choice you've taken the first step to making Soul consciousness your primary focus. This transformation only happens by choice. And faith-fueled free will is the power that turns that choice into an engine of transformation. So, make your choice a declaration; a free-will commitment towards your own transformation. I call this an Activation Phrase.

ACTIVATION PHRASE

An Activation Phrase is the substance that inspires you to build a bridge between realms and see into Soul territory. It should resonate with a profound motivation for change. Otherwise, it is a mere mental concept. It should be a clarion call to action based in deep acceptance and faith. And it should motivate you to achieve the highest and best within you.

For example, when your personality is stuck on thoughts promoting fear and anxiety and you summon the will to change, your Activation Phrase declares:

"I want to see this issue from a higher perspective."
Or "I must break this pattern of thoughts about my situation."
Or "I need to feel satisfying emotions around this problem."

To transform your personality's conditioned negative patterns, you must truly *want* it to happen, *choose* for it to happen, and do the necessary work to *make* it happen. So, a deep longing and an urgent desire for change, and an unequivocal commitment to change, are essential.

At times it can be hard to sustain your motivation. But over time, as you practice Step 4 relative to specific situations, your Activation Phrase occurs naturally, the door to Soul perspectives opens with greater ease, and spiritual insight flows effortlessly for your conscious creative use.

So, it's time to go within and consciously choose to activate change.

STEP 4: Embrace Your Thoughts—Spark a New Perspective
In Step 1, you chose a situation in your life where you are experiencing a difficulty, challenge, or dilemma. In Steps 2 and 3, you worked within the Personality Realm to identify your programmed thoughts and the overriding emotion they perpetuate.

Here, in Step 4, you will take a few still moments to embrace your thoughts and feelings to release them, and then call on your faith-fueled free will to create an "Activation Phrase" that sparks the motivation to start seeing your situation from a higher Soul perspective.

Now, let's begin.

1. Take a minute to accept and embrace all of the difficult thoughts and the core emotion you have written down. If you try to avoid them or try to push them away, you give them your life force and lose precious awareness. And they reassert their power over you.

    So, honor them as teachers and as unhealed parts of your personality. Recognize their value and purpose on your journey through life and seek their hidden gifts. Do all this with humility and compassion.

    Take a deep breath, and as you exhale, feel it RELEASE the grip your personality thoughts and emotion have had on you. Feel them melt and dissolve, the way you melt when you hug someone you love and they hug you back the same way. Embracing the disowned or rejected parts of yourself is an act of love that heals you.

    And as you do this, think, or say to yourself, "I accept and embrace all that I think and feel as a meaningful part of who I am."

2. The door is now opened to call on your own free will—to create an Activation Phrase that motivates you to rise above your conditioned personality and start to see your situation from a new perspective; to see it as an opportunity to transform your emotion into its higher state and achieve Soul growth.

    You may come up with more than one Activation Phrase, so find the one that rings truest for you in this moment. For example, in the "Dream Job" scenario, an Activation Phrase might be "It's time to see this situation in a new way!"

3. Write your phrase down on line #4 on your Broadcast Chart, the thick black horizontal line between the Personality Realm and the Soul Realm. Or note it mentally as you focus calmly within.

4. Now, *feel this phrase with your whole being!* Find and feel the motivational power and sense of relief within this phrase that makes it more than just a mental concept and gives you the hope for and determination to change.

Practicing Step 4 with humility, heartfelt sincerity, and profound intention interrupts the momentum of your conditioned personality. And in the stillness, when the interrupted personality "goes dark," you set the stage for healing communion with your Soul and can now cross the bridge to the Soul Realm where higher perspectives reside.

CHAPTER 9

Soul Thoughts & Emotions

"What lies behind us and what lies before us are tiny matters compared to what lies within us."

—Ralph Waldo Emerson

Your Soul is always supporting, counseling, guiding, and inspiring you, not only during crucial moments and decisive events, but in your ordinary day-to-day life. Its broadcasts are always in your best interest, tailored to your needs, and designed to help you grow and evolve beyond the limiting blocks and patterns of your conditioned personality.

Your Soul's broadcasts can expand your consciousness, alter the course of your life, or even save your life. It gives you urgent warnings when you're in danger, loving reassurances when you feel down, uplifting perspectives when you feel hopeless, and illuminating insights and guidance in your struggles with complex problems and murky situations.

And when you're too focused on yourself, your Soul may prompt you to offer support to others, perform acts of kindness and generosity, and even take risks for a greater purpose.

In *Soulercise* Step 5, you will practice listening for and hearing your Soul thoughts. In Step 6 you will identify an enlightened Soul emotion these thoughts perpetuate. As you follow these steps, you will see how your Soul thoughts and the emotions they elicit guide you toward wise and effective responses to difficult situations. You will learn to view challenges, crises, and even tragic life events as designed opportunities to grow and/or help others.

But, most importantly, you will cross the bridge to your Soul and develop a conscious relationship with your higher self. And this relationship is vital, because your Soul connects you to an intelligent universe and the infinite source of energy and light on this Earth plane, and in all dimensions.

HEAR YOUR SOUL THOUGHTS

A conscious, personality-transforming relationship with your higher self is a key goal of *Soulercise*. Your genuine desire and sincere, humble, persistent efforts to tune in and hear the voice of your Soul ignite this relationship.

Over time, practice and increasing Soul contact shifts your default station from your conditioned personality broadcasts to your Soul's higher perspectives. This willful relationship with your higher self opens access to higher energy frequencies and spiritual perceptions beyond the range of your automatic Personality Realm.

Most religious and spiritual teachings provide methods for building a Soul-inspired, consciousness-expanding practice—like prayer, meditation, or yoga—that cultivates a sense of peace, loving-kindness, and joy. A relationship with your Soul can be effectively built and practiced in a spiritual retreat, religious school, or meditation center where different forms of prayer, meditation, and yoga are taught over the course of a day, week, or even months.

The goal of *Soulercise* is to build upon that same Soul relationship at home and throughout the day—to maintain the peace of meditation when in the heart of life, even while faced with difficult situations. It's the mundane world that presents us with the greatest spiritual challenges, and a defining moment of enlightenment can be when someone cuts you off on the freeway or cuts in front of you in line at the supermarket.

The word "relationship" is key. Your relationship with your Soul develops in stages, just like spending time together develops friendships. To awaken this relationship, find your Soul's unique inner voice broadcasting within.

At first it may sound unfamiliar, so the best thing is to get to know its unique qualities. Often, your Soul thoughts are calmer and more relaxed than your personality thoughts. So, they reside in the distance within. The higher self is always projecting a wise, compassionate, peaceful voice while finding the benefits in any set of circumstances.

Remember: your Soul is an intelligent entity dwelling within you; your Soul is always reaching out to create a conscious, life-transforming relationship with you. But your Soul requires your will to connect and participate in this relationship. So, you must reach for your Soul. And there is no right or wrong way to connect with your higher self. Whatever method you take, you will know the Soul's voice by its qualities of peace, calm, and compassion.

Listening for Soul broadcasts is like "old fashioned" tuning into an FM radio. Imagine: You're parked alone in your car with the radio on, looking for your favorite station. Leaning forward, you slowly turn the dial, listening attentively, eyes half-closed. Then, faintly through the static, you hear your station, fading in and out. So, you lean closer, gently adjusting the dial, listening more attentively. And finally, your station comes in, clear as a bell.

Hearing your Soul broadcasts is difficult at first, because you've been so tuned in to your personality broadcasts for so long. But it gets easier over time. The more you practice, the more natural and effortless it becomes.

You "hear" your Soul's voice by turning your awareness to an inner frequency far more subtle than your personality's blaring broadcasts. It is much like listening intently through the static to find a desired radio station. But you are listening with your intuition, your spiritual ear, rather than your physical ear.

As you practice listening over time, you become more closely attuned to your Soul's vibrational frequency. Its "voice" becomes clearer, its presence becomes more palpable, and its influence in your life becomes more profound and transformative.

My twenty-minute meditation practice gives me a chance to sit quietly in my Soul's presence. When listening to my Soul's voice first thing in the morning, it sets the stage for the rest of the day. I can bring Soul consciousness into my waking state and strengthen higher perspectives of trust around a challenging situation *before* my personality hijacks my attention with distracting worries and fears.

When you listen for your Soul at the start of your day, and in random moments through the day, you begin to attune your consciousness more easily to your Soul's voice and presence.

Your Soul also "speaks" to you in dreams. So, if you lie in bed for a few minutes in the morning and tune into your dreams, you may discover important messages your Soul delivered while you slept. Because dreams occur in the Soul Realm, they can be as useful as waking experiences for your growth. Ancient religions and modern psychology agree on this point.

Betty Bethards taught that "at night we all go out of the body, we are in school, and we are taught and trained on the other side where all communication is telepathic. We spend ten days out of every month in the dream state. That is a third of our lives. Your dreams are a free tool and the easiest way in the world to get your own answers."

So, upon waking in the morning, take a few moments to quiet your mind and tune into your eternal self by meditating and/or recalling and reflecting on your dreams. Listen for the Soul's voice and presence in your meditation. Remember your dreams, reflect on the dream events, and ask your Soul to help you understand any meanings, lessons, or messages the dream conveys.

What was the dream location like? What happened? What did you do? How did you feel? All people, places, and things are a symbolic representation of you. Reflect on the dream characters: Were they male or female? What did they say or do? What did you think and feel? What messages might they be conveying?

Your dreams contain Soul teachings and revelations relating to the lessons you are here to learn. Ask your Soul to reveal your dream's meanings and messages to you and listen for insights you can apply to your life in the waking world. There are "Dream Dictionaries" and other books you can consult for additional help with understanding the messages and symbols you receive in your dreams. My "go to" dream bible is *The Dream Book* by Betty Bethards.

In your waking consciousness, your Soul can appear as a presence, a "voice," an image, a feeling, a being, an insight, or a revelation. And when you perceive your Soul in any form, you are in Soul contact and in Soul consciousness.

When your Soul appears in your conscious awareness, it's like a "Magic Eye" 3D art effect, when a hidden picture suddenly emerges from a diffuse or chaotic pattern. To experience this effect, take a minute now to reflect on the double pictures below until the hidden images appear.

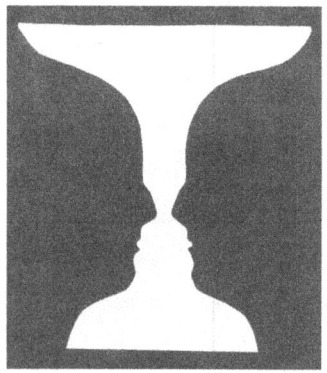 

When you looked at the first image, what initially appeared? A goblet? Or the profiles of two people? When you looked at the second picture what did you see first, the profile of a young lady wearing a feathered hat? Or an old witch with a large nose, a jutting jaw, and no teeth? Look at both pictures again until you can see their alternate images at will. It's hard at first. But it becomes easier with practice.

It's the same with your Soul. It's hard at first to perceive your Soul through the confusion and chatter of your conditioned personality. But with enough practice, it becomes second nature. And nothing compares to the feelings that come over you when your Soul suddenly appears to your conscious awareness out of the chaos of your conditioned personality.

So, start your day with the Soul-oriented practices presented here. And listen within, in random moments through the day, for your Soul's voice and presence. As you do this you become increasingly able to discern its singular voice and presence through all of the fluctuations of your personality and in all of the circumstances of your daily life.

By practicing faithfully when life is calm, you establish an anchor to steady you in difficult times. Then "solutions" to the Activation Phrase you established in Step 4 will arise gently within. And your Soul will appear in some form to guide and reassure you, like a lighthouse appearing out of the darkness to a lost or storm-tossed ship.

You'll recognize your Soul's voice through a mysterious inner knowing and drink in its loving, compassionate presence, its wise insights, its inspiring messages, its consciousness-shifting perspectives, and its life-changing revelations. And you will feel like a traveler coming home at last after a long and difficult journey.

FEEL YOUR HIGHER EMOTIONS

As you tune in to the voice of your Soul, new empowering emotions will emerge, awakening feelings of trust in your higher purpose and love for who you *really* are. The peace and presence of your Soul will bless you and those around you. You will find yourself responding to difficult situations calmly and empathetically, in a way that comforts and even inspires others.

These positive feelings and effects are spiritual food. So, try not to doubt or diminish them. Fully receive them. Savor these Soul-fruits with mindfulness and digest the spiritual nourishment they contain. And let them sustain and inspire you to persist when the tests and trials of life seem beyond your capacity. For they confirm that you are on the right path. And they reflect to you your true self—who you are in reality, in your alignment with your eternal Soul.

These two next steps in your *Soulercise* program teach you how to hear your Soul thoughts and feel your higher emotions. They are simple, but they require intention and self-awareness.

At first, your mind may tend to wander to other thoughts as you "listen" for and/or "feel" your Soul's response. Whenever your mind wanders, notice, embrace, and release your thoughts and return to listening. If you need to, restate your Activation Phrase and refocus your attention toward your Soul.

This "release and refocusing" may generate reassuring or uplifting feelings that come when you use your faith-fueled free will to realign with your Soul. You may experience a perspective shift with your issue that resolves nagging uncertainty and instills a new sense of ease and peace around it. And all of these things comprise the melody of the song your Soul is always singing within you.

PREPARATION & SOUL INQUIRY

Steps 5 and 6 are where you will tune into your Soul's broadcasts. To enhance this process, you will prepare by first entering into Relaxed Mode. Relaxed Mode uses breath exercises in preparation to connect with your internal or higher self. Before you begin, be mindful that you are preparing yourself through this exercise to ask your Soul important questions, and to hear or intuit its answers.

To prepare:

1. Sit quietly with eyes closed. Relax for a few moments by taking several deep breaths. Inhale slowly to a count of 4. Then exhale to a count of 7 and hold your breath for a

moment at the bottom of your exhale. As you do feel the energy circulating at the base of your spine.

2. Eyes still closed, continue your 4-7 breathing and focus your inner vision on your "third eye" located just above and between the eyebrows. Sense the energy circulating there. This opens the power of visualization and awakens intuition and spiritual awareness.

3. When concerns about past, present, or future issues arise, notice them without judgement. Continue your breathing and return your focus to your third eye. While sitting in Relaxed Mode, feel the stillness and peace of your breath. Continue this cycle as needed, being present to each moment as best you can, until you feel calm, relaxed, peaceful, and clear.

Now you are prepared to review your situation from a place of Soul consciousness, which dissolves your lower personality thoughts and reactions. To do this you will formulate a Soul Inquiry—a sincere request that embodies your positive intention to see the situation from a higher Soul perspective and promote inner peace.

For example, for each thought in the Personality Realm you might say: "What is another more productive perspective towards this situation?"

Or simply, "What is the opposite way to view this situation."

After formulating your Inquiry and speaking it directly while in Relaxed Mode, tune into any higher perspectives, intuitions, and visualizations that come from your Soul.

Next you will document these new Soul perspectives in the Soul Realm of your Broadcast Chart. As you do this, notice any personality thoughts that may sneak through. When they do, let them go and continue to focus on any Soul thoughts that arise.

In this step you are not just "making up" answers. You are using your lower personality thoughts to discover your Soul's higher counter-balancing perspectives. You are listening within for the higher wisdom your Soul will always broadcast. When you "hear" your Soul's response, your gut feeling or intuition, and a feeling of lightness, peace, or release will tell you, "this is my Soul's higher truth."

STEP 5: Note Soul Perspectives—Hear Your Higher Self
To begin:

1. Make an Inquiry: Read the first lower Personality Realm thought you wrote on line #1, or mentally noted. Then formulate a Soul Inquiry to help you see through and dissolve the lower thought.

2. Write an Answer: Write down the first Soul thought that comes on line #1, just above the thick black line representing the Soul Realm. Line #1 in the Soul Realm section of your Broadcast Chart corresponds to the first thought in line #1 in the Personality Realm section. If you are not writing an answer, then mentally repeat, or verbally speak the Soul thought over and over to yourself to plant it firmly in your mind.

3. Repeat this question-and-answer process with each thought you wrote down, or mentally noted, in the Personality Realm section, lines #1 - #3, and REPLACE them with your new Soul perspectives in the Soul Realm on lines #1 - #3.

In the "Dream Job" example used with Soulercise Steps 1-4, the situation was, "I didn't get the perfect job I interviewed for." The emotion was "Fear" and the first thought written down on line #1 in the Personality Realm was, "Nothing ever works out for me." The Activation Phrase for this example situation was, "It's time, I have to find a new perspective to view this!"

So now in Step 5, continuing with the same "Dream Job" scenario example, you would take a few still moments to enter Relaxed Mode and prepare to tune into a new perspective.

You would then make a Soul Inquiry asking, "What is a new way to see this situation?" Or "What is the opposite of this hopeless thought?" The thoughts you might hear and write down on line #1 in the Soul Realm might be, "When the time is right, the perfect job will come along."

Or "Don't despair, when one door shuts, another will open."

Continuing with the "Dream Job" example: Suppose you wrote angry and frustrated thoughts towards others on line #2 in the personality Realm. Such as, "Those jerks! They don't have a clue what they are doing."

Here your Soul Inquiry might be, "What is a wiser, compassionate, and more productive perspective towards others in this situation?"

Your Soul might respond with the thought, "Their rejection is no reflection on me or my ability to get hired. I wish them well." This is what you would write on line #2 in the Soul Realm section.

To continue with the "Dream Job" example: Suppose you wrote this self-critical thought about yourself on line #3 in the Personality Realm: "I'm not skilled enough, my resume sucks, and I lack experience. Who would ever want to hire me?"

Here a Soul Inquiry might be, "How can I generate healthy optimism about not getting this job?"

The Soul thoughts you hear and write down on line #3 in the Soul Realm section might be, "I am talented and have a lot to offer the right company."

Or, "I trust the universe. And it will guide me to the company I am meant to work with and the job I am meant to have."

The higher thoughts and perspectives that you write down in the Soul Realm of your Broadcast Chart guide you to be strong and to remain clear and prepared. They direct you to your path of new growth and development. And the more you tackle your problems and challenges in this way, the more you grow beyond your present capacity to the next level of Soul mastery.

Having formulated an Inquiry that embodies your positive intentions and having identified higher Soul perspectives to help you grow in understanding, strength, and wisdom, you are ready for Step 6. There you will identify the emotion your situation elicits.

STEP 6: Choose A Higher Emotion—Meet Your Opportunity

1. Turn to the Emotion List in Chapter 4. Choose an emotion from the "Opportunity" column, opposite the emotion you chose in *Soulercise* Step 3 from the "Challenge" column, regarding your situation.

    This emotion points to the Opportunity for growth you are seeking. In the current "Dream Job" example, the challenge is to transform the emotion of "Fear" relative to losing your job into the higher state of "Trust" that the future holds new opportunities for you.

2. On the top of your Broadcast Chart, under the word "Emotion," write down the "Opportunity" emotion you picked regarding your personal situation. Now consider: What color does the feeling of the emotion you picked represent for you? Write down the color that comes to you.

3. Now, take a moment and allow yourself to receive the feeling these new perspectives evoke. Feel the sense of relief and gratitude swirling within you. Feel this emotion with all your being as the energy sensations they are at the level of vibration. Where do you feel them? In your chest? Your stomach?

    Sometimes a positive emotion is difficult to maintain. Sometimes feelings of trust, security, and love have been hidden for so long that they take a while to receive and engage. That's okay. Feel instead the color that you chose. What feeling does that color generate inside you? Recognize each feeling as an energy state. And observe the ebb and flow, the passing and changing of feelings, as a living process within you.

    Now, in the depth of your being, accept this emotion as part of who you are right now. Recognize the situation as an opportunity to transform your consciousness into higher Soul states through the practice of shifting your perspective from one of Fear to one of Trust. Take a minute to relax and contemplate the situation from this perspective.

You can see here how Steps 5 and 6 are the transformative part of the *Soulercise* process.

As you formulate your Soul Inquiry, tune into your Soul, and replace your lower personality thoughts and feelings with higher

Soul thoughts and feelings on your Broadcast Chart, you align your personality with your Soul. You begin to see, with greater clarity and detail, the map of your Soul Plan charting your journey into new dimensions of your being. And the spiritual goals you came into this life to achieve progressively become realities within you.

When negative, counterproductive thoughts and emotions arise, instead of believing them or being bogged down by them, you can now *Soulercise* them. As you learn and grow and evolve through this process, these lower personality thoughts and emotions lose their power over you and you no longer believe as you once did. Now you RECOGNIZE them, RELEASE them, and REPLACE them, as you continue to grow and abide in Soul consciousness.

The more you listen within to your Soul's higher perspectives, the easier it becomes to locate and identify its singular voice and healing presence.

So, take time each day to tune into your Soul. Meditate on its wise, inspiring perspectives and watch them dissolve and replace your personality's programs. By doing this over time, you transform your personality and your life. You become a source of healing and transformation in the world.

CHAPTER 10

Soul Fitness

"I am not what happened to me, I am what I choose to become."
—Carl Jung

When you set clear intentions to replace or transform old, limiting thoughts and behaviors, you will find opportunities to turn those intentions into action. But your lower conditioned personality programs won't give up without a fight.

Your subconscious developed these programs long ago in response to formative life events that you lacked the tools or ability to manage at the time. Now they operate outside of your conscious awareness with a life and a momentum of their own that can derail even the best of intentions. And they instinctively resist all efforts to replace or transform them.

We all form numerous sub-optimal thought patterns that we don't usually notice or confront until they become troublesome for us, or intolerable for others. We all respond to familiar cues, or are triggered by stressful circumstances, and obey these default subconscious programs. At times you may feel stuck in your ways and wonder, "What does it take?"

"Why can't I change?"

"How will I *ever* get free?"

Transformation isn't achieved overnight. It takes a lot of little steps to get where you want to go. Intention is the first step. But you ultimately achieve your goals by taking action, with repetition and consistency, to achieve Soul Fitness—to continually replace your old habitual personality thoughts until they roll-over and become new, positive Soul patterns of behavior.

THE SUBCONSCIOUS MIND

Your subconscious mind is a storage and retrieval database of everything you've ever seen, felt, thought, and experienced. It stores, files, and retrieves data automatically, as needed. It behaves and responds according to countless programs neuronally coded and reinforced through repetition since childhood. This can be good and necessary or challenging and self-defeating.

On the one hand, a subconscious program is like a manufactured instinct. It enables you to function automatically and effectively, and perform with relative ease, things that required great intent, effort, and practice to learn. Every skill set relies on a subconscious program you developed in this way.

A familiar example of a positive subconscious program is learning to drive a car. First, you focus intently on a complex set of actions relative to the car, its various working parts, and your surroundings. With practice, you learn and internalize the process until it becomes second nature.

On the other hand, negative subconscious programs are like subliminal messages murmuring commands in your ear below the threshold of your conscious awareness. Ingrained since childhood by your family, society, and academia, they have tremendous power over how you think and respond.

For example, as a child you may have been told, "We can't afford it." Now you're plagued by financial issues due to a deep-seated belief that you'll never have enough money.

Or you may have been repeatedly told, "Why can't you be like your brother/sister?" Now you're hyper-competitive with your peers and respond defensively to normal feedback. Or maybe you were told, "You'll never amount to anything." Now you believe you are inferior to others and feel a constant need to prove yourself.

We've all acquired negative subconscious programs that formed specific neuronal connections in our brain that are now automatic and habitual. But there's good news. We need not be prisoners of our negative programs, doomed to forever repeat their suboptimal behaviors.

A University College of London research study showed that it takes 66 days on average for a new behavior to become an ingrained habit. The same study also showed that missing a day did not significantly diminish the overall behavior change.

So, if you slip and fall back into negative thoughts and emotions you are trying to change, don't despair, and don't judge yourself. Just start up again where you left off and keep moving toward your goal. Consistency over time is the key to making a change.

As we take action and practice new, positive Soul thoughts and behaviors, we form new neural pathways in our brain that support the new thought and behavioral patterns. These patterns gradually override and replace the old subconscious programs, and in the process, our lives are transformed. This is why you *Soulercise*.

AFFIRMATION & VISUALIZATION

In the 7th and final Step in the *Soulercise* process, you begin to reprogram your subconscious mind and transform personality thoughts and emotions with the aid of affirmation and visualization. In Steps 5 and 6 you viewed a difficult situation from your Soul's perspective, receiving inner guidance on how to proceed.

Now, in Step 7, you consciously affirm and visualize your new perspective, programing it into your subconscious mind.

A consistent affirmation and visualization practice helps turn your new perspective—your "Soul Transformation Thought"—into your new norm. When you are proficient in this personality-to-Soul reprogramming and conversion process, you can respond in the heat of difficult situations in a spontaneous, soul-guided way. And the more areas and issues you reprogram, the more Soul consciousness becomes your natural or dominant state in all situations.

Visualization is a mental rehearsal that "codes" images in your mind of your new perspective in action. You become the writer, producer, and director of your new Soul-inspired life script.

An affirmation supports your visualization with a positive statement or "code" declaring your Soul perspective to be complete and transformed. Doing this with focus and intention reprograms your subconscious mind, which cannot differentiate between what is real and what is imagined. It will manifest whatever images you create within.

In one famous study at the University of Chicago, Dr. Biasiotto divided students into three groups. He had members of each group take a basketball and do free throws as he recorded their scores. Then he had the first group practice free throws for an hour a day. He had the second group visualize shooting free throws for an hour a day but do no actual free throws. The third group did nothing.

30 days later he tested the three groups again. The third group showed no improvement. The first group that practiced actual free throws improved by 24%. But the second group that only visualized free throws also improved by 23%.

Other scientific studies have shown that visualizing a physical activity affects the body/mind in the same way as performing the physical activity. And visualizing actions in perfect form dramatically accelerates the skill-developing process.

Thomas Edison said, *"Never go to sleep without a request to your subconscious."*

Your subconscious mind operates in the background by day and takes over entirely when you are asleep. Then it has all of your brain's resources at its disposal.

As you begin to fall asleep, your Beta brainwaves, which facilitate thinking and processing, begin to turn off, and Alpha brainwaves, often called the "link between the conscious and the subconscious mind," take over. And as you progress into deep sleep, Alpha brainwaves give way to Theta and then ultimately Delta brainwaves, which activate the body's healing and growth mechanisms. Then this sequence is reversed as you begin the process of waking up.

So, your subconscious mind is the most accessible as you are going to sleep, as you begin to wake up, as well as during meditation. These times are the perfect opportunity to listen for your Soul's voice as you did in Step 5, and to practice your reprogramming affirmations and visualizations. Consistent practice effectively reprograms new Soul perspectives into your subconscious.

Visualizing who you want to be and how you want to act in

specific situations helps you to be and act this way in real life when these situations arise. Repeatedly seeing yourself positively and confidently responding to given situations helps you to respond similarly when the actual challenge presents itself.

This visualizing-in-advance method has been an essential component for decades in training professional and Olympic athletes. To prepare for a competition, Tamarin visualized her rhythmic gymnastics routines every night before falling asleep and on the morning of competition.

After her first year of doing this visualization practice, at 12 years old she became the Rhythmic Gymnastics National Champion in the Children's Division. Later she made the national team, and won medals in international competitions, just as she had visualized.

When you become proficient in this Soul affirmation and visualization process, profound shifts begin to happen. You develop new confidence and clarity relative to old problems and situations. Your Soul's perspectives, and the solutions they reveal, become your new reality. And your personality's concerns, fears, problems, and reactions wither and fade from non-use.

You will always have, and be, a personality, just as you will always have, and be, a Soul. Both aspects of your being are sacred. And each needs the other to fulfill its raison' d'être, its "reason for being", the divine purpose for which it was created.

STEP 7: Visualize/Affirm Soul Thoughts—Practice Them

Creating a new subconscious program for a difficult situation creates a new operating reality in that situation. This takes great intention and consistent practice. See yourself as an actor preparing for the role of a lifetime. You are going to study, practice, and rehearse your character until that magical shift occurs when you effortlessly *become* the character. And the character you are going to become is your own Soul.

Now, in Step 7, using the power of affirmation and visualization, you will begin to consciously exercise your Soul and anchor its higher perspectives in your daily life to build and maintain Soul Fitness. To begin:

1. Choose a Soul thought from the Soul Realm of your Broadcast Chart that best represents the higher perspective you want to use to reprogram your subconscious. Choose the thought that feels the most energizing and inspiring.

   This is your "Soul Transformation Thought," and it will be your perspective-anchor to visualize and affirm as your new reality in the problem situation. You are going to practice shifting to this Soul thought/perspective whenever the situation triggers your lower personality thoughts and emotions.

2. Close your eyes and enter Relaxed Mode— a now familiar state of relaxation.

3. With eyes still closed, visualize a large blank high-definition TV screen onto which your higher mind will project and view the images you create.

4. Now, on this screen, visualize yourself in the problem situation with as much detail as possible. See yourself in the scene as if you're part of a movie. Where are you? See the view surrounding you. Who is with you? See the person or people as clearly as you can. What tensions or emotions has the situation previously triggered in you? Feel them now.

Take a moment to contemplate your Soul Transformation Thought as you visualize the scene. See yourself and the situation from your chosen Soul perspective. Feel yourself embodying the desired qualities you are programming into your subconscious.

5. Tune in to the feeling/energy the thought contains. Feel deeply the emotion it evokes in you. Now consciously link this feeling/energy and emotion to your visualization until you feel them merge and fuse. Breathe in and internalize all these Soul-inspired elements until this perspective begins to feel true and real.

6. Create an affirmation and write it down on the "Affirmation" line on your Broadcast Chart. Then declare this new reality to be complete and manifest; that you are now the transformed, Soul-infused character in the "movie" of your actual life.

7. Repeat the above process several times, feeling the energy and emotion of this new perspective fuse into a growing sense of confidence and clarity about your situation. As you continue this practice over time, anchoring this new Soul program in your body/mind, your sense of clarity and confidence will grow into a sense of mastery that will translate into reality when you enter the situation in real life.

To further illustrate Step 7, let's complete the "Dream Job" scenario example. In this scenario, you would recall and visualize the moment you received news that you didn't get the job. You would see the scene clearly, hearing the person tell you the bad news, feeling the feelings and recalling the thoughts the news evoked in you.

Now, instead of feeling crushed and hopeless, thinking and believing that "Nothing ever works out for me," you would say your Soul Transformation Thought to yourself: "This job is not where I'm supposed to be. When the time is right, the right job will appear."

Then you would visualize yourself cheerfully making new calls to possible employers, sending out resumes with a sense of adventure, and confidently holding feelings of trust that the right job will appear in your life at exactly the right time.

Next, you would speak with conviction an affirmation that supports this visualization, confidently affirming the positive outcome to be successfully completed. You would affirm and visualize with strong intention, and trust in your life plan: "I am walking in the door on the first day of my new dream job."

You would do this until your affirmation and visualization are fully installed as a new program, and your subconscious truly believes you have succeeded.

THE TRANSFORMATION PROCESS

Now it's time to create a schedule for your practice. Every day take a few minutes—before you fall asleep, when you first wake up, in meditation, or when you notice that your conditioned personality has taken control—to do the Affirmation and Visualization process described above. Remind yourself that you are a spiritual warrior, entering the testing arena of life, armed with your Soul's transformative perspectives, power, light, and love.

And when old patterns of insecurity, fear, and stress pop up during the day, continue to apply the 7 Steps to recognize, release, and replace them with Soul thoughts that shift your emotions from uncertainty, doubt, and fear to the faith, trust, and confidence that come from a deepening connection to your Soul. As you do this practice over time, Soul consciousness will become, more and more, your present reality.

In the early and mid-stages of *Soulercising*, your conditioned personality will re-emerge as the day progresses, and the shift you experienced while doing this process will fade into the background of your consciousness the way a dream fades after waking. You may not notice right away. And again, that's okay. When you do notice, don't judge or criticize yourself. Practice patience and self-compassion.

Remember that you're human, not perfect, and start over again. Be content to begin from where you are, and to make incremental progress over time the way growth actually occurs. And as you exercise your Soul and achieve Soul Fitness, appreciate all the adventures, "mistakes," ups and downs, and learning curves along the way.

Real growth, transformation, and subconscious reprogramming takes time, practice, patience, and persistence. Beethoven didn't learn the piano overnight. And "Rome wasn't built in a day." As you persist in this practice through difficulties and challenges, you will experience growth spurts, stable plateaus, and moments of grace. Old limiting personality patterns of thought, emotion, and behavior will lose their power over you as higher Soul patterns replace them.

Then in moments of difficulty or need, miracles will happen. Situations that seemed hopeless will be unexpectedly resolved or change for the better. People will show up to help and serve you. And as you grow and change and evolve into the spiritual being you are meant to be, you will find yourself helping and serving others, and playing a part in their miracles.

IN THE HEAT OF THE MOMENT

You have now completed an entire Broadcast Chart. You've unveiled the subconscious programs behind your lower personality thoughts and the emotion they generate. And you've seen how to transform them into their higher Soul counterparts.

Take a few minutes now to read the whole chart—both the personality lines and the Soul lines. Notice the progression. See every lower personality thought and perspective as cause for transformation into higher Soul perspectives.

Now you have the knowledge and tools to strengthen your positive perspectives and transform your negative programs. So, in the "heat of the moment" in any situation, when you find yourself sinking into the emotional quicksand of fear, self-doubt, or anxiety, you can:

1. Identify the difficult situation.

2. RECOGNIZE, embrace, and accept the lower, programmed personality thoughts around your situation.

3. Consciously feel, identify, and *name* the emotion these thoughts trigger. This is your Challenge.

4. Choose an Activation Phrase, and coach yourself to RELEASE your lower personality reactions to see a higher Soul perspective.

5. Enter Relaxed Mode and tune into and REPLACE each lower personality thought about your situation with a higher Soul thought.

6. Consciously feel, identify, and *name* the new emotion that accompanies and corresponds to your higher Soul thoughts. This is your Opportunity.

7. Pick a Soul Transformation Thought. Visualize yourself responding to the situation from this new Soul perspective. Affirm the situation in its completed and transformed state.

And, when your challenging emotion presents itself in daily life, continually practice replacing your personality thoughts with your Soul Transformational Thought until its higher emotional state becomes your new norm.

Remember, self-discovery and enlightenment does not come from anything outside of you— your career, your possessions, your achievements, or your relationships. It wells up from deep inside of you. And when you know how to find these Soul qualities within, you can manifest them in every part of your life. And your life, and you, are transformed.

CHAPTER 11

Master Daily Life

"You're not going to master your life in one day. Master the day, then keep doing that every day."

–Unknown

From moment to moment, your thoughts, beliefs, and feelings *about* reality shape your perceptions *of* reality. In this sense, you do create your own reality. When you understand how your negative or lower thoughts and emotions limit and define you, you can recreate and liberate yourself into a greater higher reality, in any moment, in any situation.

When you know how to *Soulercise*, you won't be bound or defined by what you thought, felt, or did ten minutes ago, or ten years ago. Negative personality states that defeat you in one moment can be recognized and transformed in the next. You can literally start over in any moment, in any situation, from a place of Soul consciousness and master your Soul Plan while active in daily life.

But again, it's not always easy, because our lower personality thoughts and emotions are powerful and deeply ingrained. Carl Jung said, "We think we have thoughts and emotions, but really our thoughts and emotions have us."

He described being gripped by thoughts and emotions as a kind of possession. In these triggered states, we are under the influence of powerful unconscious forces. Recall a situation or event that triggered intense thoughts and emotions in you. Did you choose those thoughts and emotions? Or did they erupt with overwhelming force and possess you?

When any thought possesses you, *you* become *it*, and *it* defines *you*. Remember, your thoughts, words, and emotions emanate vibrational frequencies that reflect your present level of consciousness. Habitual thoughts and perpetuated emotions lead to actions and reactions that produce corresponding life results, for good or ill.

And understanding this cause-and-effect link—Thoughts & Emotions = Actions & Reactions = Life Results—allows you to objectively consider all perspectives and choose to develop patterns of thought and emotion that foster growth and positive change in your life.

Negative, limiting thoughts and emotions don't have to trap you in lower versions of yourself. When you know how to *Soulercise*, they actually become fuel for further self-knowledge, growth, and Soul evolution. When they arise, you can spot them and observe them with loving self-acceptance. In each moment you can choose to replace them with inspiring thoughts and emotions that conduct the power of your Soul and manifest your Soul's vision for this lifetime.

THE GIFT OF LOVE

As a human being on this Earth, you have a life purpose—you go to school, you may get married, raise kids, and/or make a wonderful living, but it's not your sole reason for being in this lifetime.

As an embodied Soul, you also have your own higher purpose for inhabiting a physical body. Your higher purpose is revealed each day, each moment when you bring the knowledge of Soul consciousness into daily life, and you give and receive love to yourself while mastering your Soul Plan.

Remember, as an embodied personality in this temporary school of life on Earth, you will make mistakes and experience setbacks. And these are all part of your curriculum.

So, don't be too hard on yourself. Give yourself the gift of love. Love is the "eternal attitude" of the Soul. And when we learn to love ourselves the way our Soul, our higher angelic Guides, and other Beings of Light love us, we support the fulfillment of our true potential.

But even love takes practice. Forgive yourself and learn to laugh at yourself when you slip up. Celebrate when you succeed and do well. Love and accept yourself as you are, while aiming to excel in all you do. When you're lost, confused, or need help, ask for guidance, and you will receive the tools you need to solve present problems and bring about lasting change.

Practicing love towards yourself and others will support you through the challenges of the transformation process. And as it heals your relationship with yourself, you will feel the peace of coming home *to* yourself at last. And you'll be comfortable in your own skin in a way you've never been before. Over time, the love and Soul consciousness that you truly desire will become your natural state in this realm as it is in realms beyond.

The remarkable visionary and founder of Hay House Publishing, Louise Hay, once said, "I have come to this planet to learn to love myself more, and to share that love with all those around me."

Louise passed away in 2017, but her inspirational teachings on giving love live on. Louise taught: "Life is a voyage of self-discovery. To me, to be enlightened is to go within and to know who and what we really are, and to know that we have the ability to change for the better by loving and taking care of ourselves. Love is something we can choose, the same way we choose anger, or hate, or sadness. It's always a choice within us. Let's begin right now in this moment to choose love. It's the most powerful healing force there is."

For access to Louise Hay's books, affirmations, and exceptional teachings visit www.louisehay.com

Again, there is no practice more important than observing your personality thoughts and behaviors with loving kindness—with a compassionate and caring attitude. When you can do this with yourself, you can do it with others.

It may be difficult to feel self-love in the early stages of your *Soulercise* practice. And even when you've made progress, you may fall back into old habitual personality patterns. Adding additional and powerful affirmations of unconditional love to your daily routine will help with this.

It's important to note that loving affirmations bear fruit when you put them into action. So, *sincerely* practice loving and compassionate thoughts and tangible loving actions toward yourself.

Spend a minute or two each morning looking into your eyes in the mirror. See and feel your beautiful and mysterious Soul looking out at you from your own eyes. Talk to yourself kindly, face to face.

Reflect on your life, and acknowledge and praise yourself with love, admiration, and compassion for making it this far in life. Become your biggest cheerleader and your own best friend.

Most importantly, love and encourage yourself as you might lovingly encourage a child who needs your support, guidance, and care. When fear or anxiety arise in you, speak lovingly to yourself. Tell yourself, "Even though these fearful thoughts reside within me, I completely love and accept myself." Then feel the sense of love permeate your being as the fear begins to dissolve.

When love is the basis of your relationship to yourself, your thoughts and feelings align with love and produce the effects that only love can produce in your life. When you cross over into the presence of your divine teachers and guides, there is only love. So, while you work to master daily life, give the gift of love to yourself and others while you gain knowledge here, in this lifetime.

Each moment you do this, the potent feeling and vibrational energy of love dissolves and releases past conditioned perceptions. This automatically aligns your personality with your Soul and supports your growth as you walk your path through daily life.

THE STORIES YOU TELL

Not only are we eternal Souls temporarily residing in physical bodies, but we also have powerful brains wired to explore, investigate, understand, learn, and grow. We're here today because for 2.5 million years, our ancestors survived by their wits, will, vision, and spirit as they evolved, subdued, and "civilized" their own primitive natures, and made the world the more just and habitable place that we have inherited.

Now it's our turn to continue the grand evolutionary journey, and to do what we can in our own lives to make the world a little better than the one we were born into. This is a noble goal, and a grand story to live by. It reveals the meaning and purpose of the past and the present. And it inspires us to help create a better future by improving ourselves and contributing to the greater good of all.

We humans have always told, lived, and made sense of the world through stories. And we're always telling stories whether we know it or not. Listen for the stories you tell yourself with your thoughts and beliefs. Do they weaken you or empower you? Do they motivate and activate you, or dishearten or paralyze you? Do they fill you with hope, love, enthusiasm, and joy? Or fear, anger, bitterness, and despair?

Soulercise uncovers the tracks laid down by stories we tell ourselves, believe, and live by. These stories shape our perceptions and our worldview. They influence our attitudes, choices, and actions/inactions. And they direct the course of our lives, often without our realizing it. We "hear" these stories every hour of every day on our personality and Soul broadcasts. But we don't always hear them consciously or intentionally.

It's important to know what your stories are and how they affect you. Because you are only as happy, healthy, resilient, and wise as the stories you tell yourself about yourself, your life experiences, your world, and the universe you inhabit. Einstein was pointing to this when he wrote: "The most important decision every person must make is whether he lives in a friendly or a hostile universe."

Einstein clearly knew that a friendly universe brings out the best in everything. So, what universe do you live in? It depends on which story, and which storyteller, you are listening to.

As you know, there are two storytellers: The unpredictable narrator—your conditioned personality—whose lower, negative stories weaken and discourage you. And your Soul, the Master Storyteller, whose stories strengthen, inspire, and uplift you and bring out the best in you. When things are tough and life is stressful, stop and ask yourself, "Hmm…which story am I choosing now?"

No matter what difficult situations you encounter, the bottom line is that as a Soul, you can create a new story for any challenge you encounter.

It's okay to get angry over the actions or reactions of those around you, or sad and fearful about a serious family situation. But no matter what injustice or trauma you may have to endure, as soon as you fall into the habit of blaming anyone (including yourself) or letting the "doom and gloom" in, you become locked into a story you are telling yourself and trapped in lower personality states.

Forgive others and yourself for the sake of your own healing and freedom. Find new stories to live by during your brief sojourn on this Earth plane and move forward in your own evolution.

LIFE REVIEW

In Carl Jung's final interview with BBC News in 1959, a reporter asked him if he believed that life went on after the death of the body. "I don't believe," Jung said emphatically, remembering his own near-death experience. "I know!"

Near-Death Experiences (NDEs) have been reported throughout history, with around 200,000 NDEs reported each year. In the last 50 years, dozens of researchers like Raymond Moody, Elizabeth Kubler Ross, and Kenneth Ring have interviewed hundreds of thousands of NDE survivors.

The massive body of NDE literature, as well as documented experiences of after-death communication (ADC) with departed loved ones, and even my own trauma-induced out-of-body experience (OBE), support the assertion of mystics down through the ages that: *There is no death!*

Countless NDE accounts describe the Soul separating from the body, near-instantaneous life reviews, entering the presence of spiritual beings and being asked, or asking oneself—with compassion, not judgement: "Did I fulfill my Soul plan?"

"How much growth did I accomplish?"

"What did I contribute?"

"How much love did I give and receive?"

And most who have had NDEs report returning to Earthly life with profound and positive changes of perspective and a new vision of life, or even a new higher purpose.

But you don't have to experience an NDE or wait until you "die" to do a life review. That same Soul intelligence is within you now. So, make time each day to strengthen your connection to your Soul. Examine and reflect on your life while you're here in a body. Ask yourself: "Are my habitual thoughts, actions and behaviors aligned with my Soul?"

"Am I on my path, fulfilling my higher purpose, and accomplishing what I came here to do?"

"Am I cultivating the light of my Soul in my life and shining it into the lives of those around me?"

Soulercise is as important for your Soul as exercise is for your body. Set aside some time at the end of each day to perform a life review. Pause, reflect, and review what happened during the day.

What challenges or difficulties did you experience? What thoughts and emotions were triggered? How did you do in the heat of those moments? Did you use them as opportunities to practice? If not, take a few moments, visualize what happened and love yourself for it, tune into your Soul, and *Soulercise* those triggered thoughts and emotions retroactively.

EVERYDAY SCENARIO

Difficult situations can run the gamut from mundane and routine to traumatic and life-altering. But the potential and purpose of every difficult or even annoying situation is to practice Soul mastery in the moment.

Consider this routine scenario: You start your day by connecting to your Soul first thing in the morning. You feel clear, energized, inspired, and ready to meet the world. You take a few still moments to anchor your Soul Transformation Thought in your consciousness and say your Affirmation. Then you get out of bed, get dressed, have breakfast, and walk out the door. Your day is busy, demanding, and productive. And by the end of the day, you're exhausted.

On your way home, you stop to pick up some groceries for dinner. You find yourself standing in a check-out line with the world's slowest cashier. He scans items in slow-motion, talking and joking with each customer. He's clearly in no hurry, but you are. And five people are in front of you. Tired, hungry, and in a hurry, your personality kicks in with a frustrating story about the situation.

"Dammit! I've been working all day! I'm tired. I just want to get home! And this idiot is just standing around gabbing and wasting everyone's time! Who does he think he is, a comedian?"

"Ah geez, this is ridiculous."

On and on and on it goes. And you fall for it.

Welcome to the domain of your conditioned personality. You're in its grip now, but you can't bring yourself to acknowledge it. Your irritated personality finds it more satisfying to indulge in mental tantrums rather than humble itself, take responsibly, and do the work required to transform its reactive thoughts and emotions.

As your irritation drains your energy and "dims your light," you consider taking your groceries and moving to another cashier. Then you notice the nudge your Soul has been giving for the last few minutes. It's asking you, "Is this moment of escalating frustration worth sacrificing the higher joy of Soul consciousness? What path are you on and what story are you telling and living right now?"

You stop, notice what is happening, and ask yourself, "What lesson can I learn from this situation?"

And you choose to *Soulercise*, right there in line.

You recognize your annoyed thoughts, the emotion you are perpetuating, and you identify your lesson in this lifetime—to transform frustration into contentment and anger into stillness. Take a minute to accept and embrace your thoughts about the situation and the core emotion of frustration you are feeling.

Then take several slow deep breaths, holding your exhale for a few moments while feeling peaceful energy and light wash over you, dissolving your frustration while you continue to stand in line.

Remembering that your Soul's higher thoughts are the guiding light on your life path, you now create a Soul Inquiry, "What is a better way to view this situation?"

You then listen for the higher Soul perspectives that rise within.

Now you replace your frustrated personality thoughts with kind and compassionate Soul thoughts that connect you spiritually to the cashier. You see that he is, after all, another spiritual being on Earth like yourself, trying to do his best in the situation he is in. Feeling this new perspective, you think, "I will get home when I am supposed to be there. This guy is doing his best. Who knows what hardships he's dealing with in his life? I wish him well."

When you do this process with heartfelt sincerity, you fulfill Plato's directive: "Be kind, for everyone you meet is fighting a hard battle."

You make a shift from personality to Soul consciousness, and your Soul bonds with their Soul. Buddhists call this "right relationship," and Christians call it "blessing."

Congratulations! You've let go of your personality's agendas and reactions and entered the domain of your Soul while standing in a supermarket check-out line. You've realized that getting home on time for dinner is less important than who you are being each moment, and less important than your right relationship to those Souls whose paths you cross each day.

When you align with your Soul and enter into "right relationship" with people and events in this way, your transformation releases "blessing" power into the situation. And miracles can happen.

Best of all, this alignment transforms anger and frustration into stillness and contentment which is what you came into this lifetime to accomplish—the challenging emotions you came here to master.

On another note, that entire story is actually mine. At the start of that day, after my morning meditation, I prayed to be led to solutions for my daughter's desperate medical situation. I went to the market, exhausted after a long day at work, and the cashier was behaving exactly as described in the above example. I stood in line, irritated and grumbling to myself.

As I was about to change lines, I recognized my challenging emotion, and it stopped me cold. I realized I had two choices: I could continue my internal lower personality frenzy, or I could *Soulercise* the situation and be restored to Soul consciousness. I chose the latter. I took a few deep breaths, and told myself, "Okay, here's my lesson, let's practice!" I became truly present, relaxed, and in "right relationship" as I followed the 7 Steps.

Then the woman in front of me took a magazine from her cart and returned it to the rack. As she did, the title of the cover article caught my eye. It was written by a professional on the very matter I'd been praying about that morning! I bought the magazine. And the article directed me to the exact resource that provided the help and guidance my daughter needed. My morning prayer had been answered!

My personality saw the cashier as an irritating obstacle on my path home. But my shifting into to Soul consciousness revealed him to be the vehicle through which the universe was able to reach and teach me. Had the cashier been faster, I may not have noticed the magazine randomly tossed onto the newsstand. Had I remained in my personality state, I might have gone to a different cashier and missed the answer altogether.

When you enter Soul consciousness, you perceive, feel, and understand things beyond the scope of your personality. You recognize the spiritual universe looking out at you from the eyes of everyone you meet, speaking to you and teaching you in every situation and event in your life on Earth. You pay closer attention to subtle signs, messages, and inner whisperings.

And as you do, doors open, people and circumstances appear

that serve your highest good, and all the things you truly need flow freely toward you.

So, yes, the Earth is one of the finest schools in the universe, perfectly designed to teach, test, and develop you to the highest possible level in accordance with your Soul plan. The difficult experiences you designed to learn and grow, are your magnificent opportunities to master daily life and expand into the higher Soul states you seek.

To reiterate what the Beings of Light taught during my out-of-body experience:

"In one mortal lifetime, you will attempt to master two or three challenging emotions. So, take time each day to go within, charge your system, and cultivate the power of Soul consciousness."

"Observe yourself in daily life. Get to know who you are. And in the face of difficulties, choose who you want to be."

Now, *that's* exciting!

CHAPTER 12

The Brain Connection

"The brain is a muscle that can move the world."
—Stephen King

In the mid-19th century, the great American philosopher Ralph Waldo Emerson said, "You are what you think, all day long."

In the last few decades, neuroscientific studies conducted around the world have validated Emerson's philosophical assertion. Using cutting-edge technologies to track the movement of thoughts through the brain, these studies seek to answer questions like: "Where do thoughts emerge from, and how are they produced?"

"Exactly how do thoughts affect our biochemistry and our behaviors?"

And "What is the mechanism by which the brain mediates and facilitates our thoughts, behaviors, and personalities?"

Think of the brain as the "hardware" of the body, a circuit board of neural connections. The human brain weighs around three pounds and contains as many as 100 billion cells called

The Brain Connection

neurons. Each of these neurons can connect to at least 1,000 other neurons, so the brain may have at least 100 trillion connections in all. Every second, a single neuron may send as many as 1,000 signals that can move from neuron to neuron at speeds of up to 250 miles per hour!

Stable brain signals and neural connections make everything you do and work for in life possible. They facilitate the memory, focus, and concentration you need to function at optimal levels. They allow you to *Soulercise* and "recode" your conditioned thoughts and emotions. But if, for one reason or another, your neural signals and connections become fundamentally unstable, the resulting brain dysregulation likely prevents you from functioning at optimal levels and achieving lifetime goals.

Unstable neural signals and connections can negatively affect you in many ways, a few of which can be either hyperactive or fatigued brain function.

A hyperactive brain—neurons firing too fast—can generate uncontrollable thoughts and emotions. This can be distracting, disturbing, and anxiety-provoking.

A fatigued or weakened brain—neurons firing too slow or not at all—can diminish your memory, attention, concentration, and motivation. Both conditions make it hard to function effectively.

The good news is that you're not stuck with your brain's present limitations. There are steps you can take to find the source of your symptoms and restore diminished cognition, improve memory, heal injuries, relieve anxiety, and enhance your overall brain function. If you want to improve your present situation and live a life filled with energy, inspiration, and motivation, a NeuroFitness program is an optimal solution.

NEUROFITNESS AND QEEG

6.4 million American children ages 4–17 have been diagnosed with ADHD. 4% of Americans, 18 years or older, deal with the effects of ADHD on a daily basis. 6.3 million Americans live with the after-effects of head/brain injuries. Many more suffer undiagnosed diminished cognitive function.

The following symptoms may be signs of brain dysregulation:

- Insomnia
- Short term memory problems
- Difficulty concentrating or sustaining focus for long periods of time
- Difficulty calming a racing mind or letting go of thoughts
- Mental confusion
- Disorientation
- Sensitivity to light and sound
- Inexplicable bouts of fatigue, anger, or apathy

However, just like you exercise to build a better body, you can exercise to build a better brain and relieve presenting symptoms. With a comprehensive NeuroFitness program, you can transform your brain and your life. When your brain is optimized, you sleep soundly, complete tasks and projects, organize your thoughts, and face major life challenges with greater ease.

Often called an "invisible disability," brain injury, especially an older head whiplash, can go undetected and perpetuate resulting symptoms for many years. When you break your arm you know immediately, and an x-ray will show the location and extent of the break. Also, a cast at the targeted location not only aids in bone healing, but also makes the injury visible to others. When you wear a cast, no one is going to ask you to help move furniture.

With subtle brain injuries and other dysregulations, however, you often appear "normal," and people expect you to function normally. And if you can't, it can become socially, psychologically, and professionally problematic.

But wait! Here's the good news. The latest technological advancements in neuroscience and computer science not only provide an easily accessible view into the brain, but they also make invisible disabilities, visible, so they can be healed.

A QEEG or quantitative EEG, often called a Brain Map, will show the location and extent of brain dysregulations. Simply using an amplifier attached to a cap with electrodes that have been placed on your head, technicians can record the electrical activity of your brain. Once the data is recorded and then analyzed, a QEEG report is then printed out and reviewed with you.

A trained professional can pinpoint specific regions in your brain where it is overactive, underactive, or stuck in a sub-optimal pattern. Most importantly, you can see the source of any symptoms you may be experiencing.

A growing number of clinicians around the world are using QEEG like an "x-ray" to then develop a NeuroFitness program.

Utilizing custom-built protocols, the dysregulated neural pathways identified in your Brain Map can be targeted and trained. With repetition and consistency, just like going to the gym regularly will build stronger muscles, a NeuroFitness program will strengthen weakened connections, heal injured neurons, optimize problematic or debilitating symptoms, and even make a "good" brain great.

Whether you are eight years old or eighty, you can train your brain to rewire and heal itself!

Numerous studies show that the brain's neuroplasticity—its ability to regenerate itself and recover from strokes, brain injuries, and more—allows it to physically change as a result of interaction with technology. The brain possesses a remarkable capacity at any age to reorganize networks and even heal white matter damage, especially with the assistance of "brain training" hardware.

Even without the aid of evolving technologies, there are many cases of adults who suffered massive strokes and were able to regain functioning. One man who lost an entire brain hemisphere and all its functions regained those functions by forming new neural pathways in the opposite hemisphere.

So, your brain is not bound to its current condition. And you are not doomed to live within the limits of your genetic inheritance or suffer irreversible cognitive decline.

Brain cells do die off as you age, but you continue to grow new neurons into your eighties. And your brain's amazing neuroplasticity means that, with sufficient motivation, determination, and the right technologies, you can "upgrade" your brain at any age. Bottom line, you can build a better brain if you put the time and effort into it.

A QEEG and NeuroFitness program using the latest neurotechnology is invaluable for developing and maintaining a healthy, well-functioning brain. The phrase, "Use it or lose it," applies here. Better yet, it also increases your ability to access higher states of consciousness and maximize the benefits of *Soulercise* practices.

CROSS-TRAIN YOUR BRAIN—THE COMMON

Systems that help you build a better brain are comprised of methods to develop energy and sustain resilience in your body, tools to strengthen the power of your mind, and most importantly,

technology to train the activity of your brain. The following commonly known elements in a good "Cross-Train Your Brain" program have been in existence for centuries:

Physical exercise and complex physical movements

Numerous studies show that regular exercise enhances brain fitness, uplifts your mood, stimulates blood circulation, and much more. Studies show that complex physical movements —think dance, martial arts, and tai chi—or activities that involve synchronized arm and leg movements—think walking and juggling—balance the left and right hemispheres of your brain and bring you into higher states of creativity and awareness.

It's no coincidence that great writers like Mark Twain, Walt Whitman, Ralph Waldo Emerson, and Frederick Nietzsche did much of their creative thinking and problem solving while taking long walks.

Healthy diet, vitamins, and supplements

Our compromised food system contains less vitamins and minerals than it did thirty years ago, and numerous unhealthy and toxic ingredients that were not in our food system fifty years ago. It's all not great news for your brain and your body.

Every time you eat conventional processed or non-organic food, you may also be consuming body and brain-ravaging ingredients like chemical fertilizers, pesticides, preservatives, flavor enhancers, artificial coloring, antibiotics, growth hormones, genetically modified glutens, mercury, aluminum dioxide, and more.

Comprehending the labels on many food products today requires a chemistry degree. Also, studies show that our compromised and often contaminated food system is related to a dramatic increase in heart disease, auto-immune disorders, dementia, obesity, and a host of other ailments.

And due to our vitamin and mineral-deficient food system, quality vitamins and supplements are absolutely necessary to make up the balance.

So, to enhance your body and brain, eat organic foods and take quality nutrients and supplements that feed and nourish your brain and reduce inflammation.

Reading substantive, thought provoking material

Reading, reflecting, and comprehending are three activities that exercise and stimulate the brain. So read something substantive for at least twenty minutes each day. Ask to be guided to a book that enlightens and informs you. You'll learn new things that can open new avenues and possibilities in your life. And you and your brain will reap the benefits.

Self-regulation techniques

Self-regulation skills enable us to manage our attention, perspectives, thoughts, emotions, moods, and behaviors. They develop and refine our self-awareness, our emotional intelligence, and our ability to cope with the stresses of life. The ability to relax under pressure, release stress, return to center, and experience regenerative equanimity is essential in our increasingly stressful world.

Self-regulation skills are great for your brain, your body, your mind, and your goals. They can slow down or prevent cognitive decline and add years to your life.

Consider this definition of self-regulation from *Psychology Today*:

"Research consistently shows that self-regulation skill is necessary for reliable emotional wellbeing. Behaviorally, self-regulation is the ability to act in your long-term best interest, consistent with your deepest values. (Violation of one's deepest values causes guilt, shame, and anxiety, which undermine wellbeing.) Emotionally, self-regulation is the ability to calm yourself down when you're upset and cheer yourself up when you're down."

Self-regulation skills should be taught to every child starting in kindergarten. But they rarely are. One notable exception is MindUP™ www.mindup.org, a signature program of the Goldie Hawn Foundation, established in 2003 in Los Angeles.

Based firmly in neuroscience, the mission of the MindUP program is: "to help children develop the knowledge and tools they need to manage stress, regulate emotions, and face the challenges of the 21st century with optimism, resilience, and compassion."

CROSS-TRAIN YOUR BRAIN – THE INNOVATIVE
In addition to the above centuries-old list of more commonly known elements in a good brain wellness program, complementary and highly advanced brain technologies have evolved over the last few decades and are becoming more well-known. You can now readily find a practitioner in your area who provides services such as QEEG brain maps and personalized brain training programs.

NeuroFit is now a part of Jyzen, the most advanced bio-optimization facility on Earth. Go to www.jyzen.com to learn about the vast array of services Jyzen and Dr. Beth McDougall provide. There you will also find further details on the following advanced elements of an effective NeuroFitness program:

Neurofeedback, Neurostimulation, and Photobiomodulation

Brain training is becoming increasingly feasible. Various neurotechnologies enhance the brain's ability to change the way it functions and provide customized protocols that promote healthier brain function and reduce or eliminate unwanted symptoms.

The first step in any Brain Training program is getting a QEEG "brain map" that details the specific regions, neural hubs, and electrical frequency bands that are dysregulated in your particular brain. Then a personalized training plan can be created that applies the following neurotechnologies:

Neurofeedback uses operant conditioning methods to measure the electrical activity of brainwaves and provide a feedback signal or "reward" (visual or auditory) to the brain so it can heal itself through neuroplasticity. Several resources for both a QEEG and neurofeedback training are:

- Brainmaster: www.brainmaster.com
- Neuroguide: www.appliedneuroscience.com
- NeuroField: www.neurofieldneurotherapy.com

Neuromodulation, also known as *Neurostimulation*, uses a customized blend of pulsed Electromagnetic Field (pEMF), transcranial Alternating Current and Direct Current (tACS) (tDCS), and transcranial Random Noise and Pink Noise (tRNS) (tPNS) methods to influence the brain to regulate specific pathological brainwave patterns. A resource for Neuromodulation/Stimulation is NeuroField Neurotherapy, Inc: www.neurofieldneurotherapy.com and www.neurofield.org.

Photobiomodulation (PBM), or light therapy, uses visible red and invisible near infrared (NIR) light methods to stimulate and revitalize the brain's energy sources (mitochondria) and increase connectivity and blood flow in the brain to improve cognitive performance. A resource for Photobiomodulation is Vielight: www.vielight.com.

All the above companies manufacture hardware and software now used by clinicians all over the world to help you build a better brain.

EWOT and Vasper

EWOT, or Exercise With Oxygen Therapy, uses the body's heart and lungs to deliver as much oxygen to your brain as possible. When the heart, lungs, and brain circuits are active as in exercise, the increased blood flow carries the oxygen to the deep recesses of the brain and promotes healing. A well-oxygenated brain makes you feel calm, relaxed, and mentally clear, and helps heal the emotional and cognitive decline resulting from head injuries. An excellent resource is LiveO2: www.liveO2.com.

VASPER maximizes the effects of rehabilitation through exercise and is an awesome 21-minute workout. VASPER expedites recovery after injury by combining the elements of:

- *Compression* – to quickly build up lactic acid, mimicking the effect of an hour-long workout in 21 minutes and triggering a systemic recovery response, including the natural release of anabolic hormones.
- *Interval training/circulation* – to optimize blood flow/blood oxygen levels and maximize the body and the brain's self-healing potential.
- *Liquid cooling* – to mitigate stress and fatigue and maintain high levels of oxygen throughout the body and the brain.

For more information visit www.jyzen.com and/or www.vasper.com.

HRV

HRV, or Heart Rate Variability training, teaches you to regulate your involuntary nervous system, which controls your heart rate. This is important because your heart signals, or patterns of variability, significantly effect brain function. Erratic patterns inhibit emotional processing and higher cognitive functioning, diminishing the ability to think clearly and manage stress. Stable HRV patterns facilitate cognitive function and reinforce emotional stability. An HRV resource is HeartMath, www.heartmath.com.

Mindfulness Training

Mindfulness is the process of focusing your attention on the present moment of experience while calmly accepting your thoughts and feelings. Practicing mindfulness has been linked to positive changes in the brain, especially in the amygdala, which manages "fight or flight" and stress responses.

Soulercise deploys the same mindfulness skills that affect positive changes in your brain. And there are other self-regulation practices worth doing to extend your cognitive and emotional well-being such as:

- Tapping: www.thetappingsolutionfoundation.org
- Brainspotting: www.brainspotting.com
- The Emotion Code: www.discoverhealing.com

MEDITATION

Meditation has been practiced for thousands of years. Originally it was meant to deepen one's understanding of the sacred and mystical forces of life. More recently, meditation has also become a means for relaxation and stress reduction.

There are many ways to meditate. You don't have to spend hours in the lotus posture, silently chanting a mantra (unless that is your practice). It can be as simple as a twenty-minute daily routine, sitting in a chair or lying on a mat or bed. But no matter what form of meditation you choose, a regular meditation practice, once or twice a day, morning and/or evening, produces profound results.

A consistent meditation practice will calm your mind, relax your nervous system, lower your blood pressure, charge your electrical field, strengthen your body's immune system, and more.

Additionally, in the quiet of meditation, your Soul will often manifest to you as a peaceful, healing presence, a meaningful idea, a deep insight, or a profound feeling or emotion of love, gratitude, or joy. There's nothing better than meditation to help you manage the challenges of daily life on Earth.

A consistent meditation practice also initiates beneficial changes in your brain. After more than ten years of analyzing QEEG brain maps, I can easily see the effects of stress/trauma on the brain. When reviewing an EEG recording, I first look at the regions of the brain connected to the amygdala—the "fight or flight"/fear response —to determine the levels of stress/trauma.

When this area of the brain is severely dysregulated, it correlates to a subjective experience of trauma that has impacted the autonomic nervous system and requires training to return to a healthy regulated state.

But the positive effects of meditation on the brain weren't obvious to me at first. I discovered this phenomenon when anomalies began to appear in these predictive amygdala trauma patterns. In several cases, I'd complete the EEG analysis thinking, "This client has a stable history."

Then, during the consult, they'd describe living in fear as a kid because their mother chased them around the house with a butcher knife, or their alcoholic father was verbally and physically abusive, or tragedy disrupted and destabilized their lives.

These anomalies of people with traumatic histories having balanced amygdala patterns in their brain maps was puzzling at first. Then I recalled how meditation had helped to heal my life traumas, and I started asking these clients, "Do you meditate?"

To this day, in 100% of these cases, the answer is, "Yes."

And, quite often they began meditating as a very young adult. It's then rewarding for clients to see their regulated amygdala network connections as compared to similar trauma situations without meditation, and to know that their efforts to meditate have made a huge difference.

Similar healing patterns have recently shown up in the QEEG brain maps of individuals with a trauma background, but who have also had a close relationship with animals such as horses, dogs, and cats.

Research has confirmed that equine therapy lowers blood pressure and heart rate, and these brain maps are proof of that. A loving relationship with animals, especially horses but dogs and cats as well, helps to regulate your nervous system and turns off the "Amygdala Switch," letting your brain and body know you are "safe" now. It automatically puts you in a calm meditative state that is ultimately healing.

Meditation's beneficial effects on the brain are well documented in numerous studies over decades by researchers like Jeff

Tarrant Ph.D. at the NeuroMeditation Institute, LLC. www.neuromeditationinstitute.com.

If you already have a meditation practice in place, awesome! If you are new to meditation, there are many kinds to choose from and teachers to learn from. Jeff Tarrant's teachings on styles of meditation and yoga are a great resource, and his book, *Meditation Interventions to Rewire the Brain,* is available on Amazon.

Also, Betty Bethards' easy to follow 5-Step meditation process www.innerlight.org/page6.html, is a simple, easy to follow technique channeled by her teachers. Through her books, lectures, and Inner Light Foundation, Betty taught how to "connect to the core of the Earth and the top universe."

By clasping your hands for the first ten minutes, you bring energy in and let it charge up your system, then by opening your palms up for the second ten minutes, you let the energy flow out through your fingertips into your magnetic field and then out into the universe. And lastly, by closing your fists just before finishing, you set your intentions with affirmation and visualization.

There's no one "right" or "best" meditation practice. Ask and trust your Soul to guide you to the meditation practice that's "right" and "best" for you. When a meditation practice is added to your daily routine, it's amazing how your energy levels increase and your brain functions more effectively to maintain Soul consciousness in the face of Earthly challenges.

ENERGY AND LIGHT

What is known as the "life force" is the scientifically proven electrical magnetic field or energy system that surrounds all living things. Within this system surrounding the human body are the vortices of energy (chakras) that also vibrate at lower or higher frequencies depending on the level of blockage or clearance within your energy system.

A clear and high vibrating life force makes you alive, alert, and present, while a blocked and low vibrating field results in sluggishness, mental fatigue, and emotional dysregulation.

The quality and quantity of your energy system is directly affected by your will to routinely increase and maintain your electromagnetic field. A conscious effort to enhance your life force will keep your energy high and your battery charged. It will improve your mental capacity/brain fitness, influence emotional stability, and solidify your efforts to face your challenges and program all you need to enter your life.

There are many teachers within organized religions and many meditation and healing techniques around the world that expound upon this notion of life force and energy, providing teachings that promote its enhancement. Most recently, I was led to Dana Duryea who offers techniques for "Running Energy" at the Foundation for Spiritual Development in San Rafael, CA. www.beingatcause.org.

We are all electrical beings in need of grounding and holding space to "charge our systems and maintain the power of Soul consciousness" as the Beings of Light had said.

When your energy is low and blocked, not only do you lack the fuel to function optimally, but also negative personality thoughts tend to prevail and feed challenging emotions such as fear and anxiety. This ultimately "drains your battery" and can lead to excessive eating, drinking, or even physical breakdown and illness.

When your energy is high and clear, you operate as a fine-tuned machine running on all cylinders. Negative thoughts give way to new Soul perspectives, promoting emotions of trust and peace.

This keeps your "battery charged" and gives you the fuel and focus required to approach rather than avoid your life.

Most importantly, a clear and high energy field attracts like-minded people to you, brings the help you need, and allows you the chance to live with love, patience, and compassion for yourself and others while achieving your goals for this lifetime.

As you work to increase your energy and light, it's also important to appreciate that shifts toward Soul consciousness come in cycles and rhythms. So, honor the cycles of your body, energy levels, and emotions. Understand that cycles of difficulties and lulls in energy do not last forever.

The periods of difficulty and lulls in your energy are an important part of your self-discovery journey. They are the gifts that are given to move you forward on your path toward enlightenment and ensure that during this short time on Earth you accomplish what you came here to do.

The opportunity now is to increase your energy and light while transforming your thinking at each level of experience *until both your thinking and your experience change.*

THE POWER OF VICTORY

Your Soul knows that life always serves your highest good, no matter how difficult your situation seems in the moment. With *Soulercise*, this understanding becomes your personal truth and guiding light. It shifts your relationship with all the situations, events, and people you encounter on your path to the greater good and redefines your relationship to life itself.

Paramahansa Yogananda described this in the following excerpt from his talk, "To be Victorious in Life:" "You can go as far as you want to go, past all limitations, and live a supremely victorious existence. You have all the power to accomplish what you want."

With the 7 Steps, you now know how to become a Soul seeker and use the power of mind to master your higher purpose. Your brain is now fit to achieve the victory that lies on the other side of every struggle instead of focusing on thoughts about the struggle itself.

With your completed Broadcast Charts, you'll have identified the emotions you came to master and can track your progress in real-time. This will help you to stay current, grounded, and on point while feeling the peace of being on your path.

As you apply what you've learned, you build bridges to your Soul. You spend more time in Soul consciousness, and the qualities of your Soul now increasingly inform, guide, and characterize your human personality.

And, by raising the vibratory rate of your energy field, you align your brain and body with the highest powers of the universe. Higher spiritual frequencies become reliable sources of guidance, inspiration, healing, and transformation while on your Soul journey.

Most importantly, as you complete your Soul plan and pass on from this life, the same divine forces that guided you here on Earth, and even your loved ones who've transitioned, draw you to higher frequencies on the "other side" and celebrate your victories with you.

Fortunately, this revelry goes both ways. You, too, can celebrate your loved ones' victories once they've crossed through the veils of death. I know I eventually managed to do so. After Tamarin passed on, I wanted to celebrate her victories as well as grieve for her. So, once again, I enlisted the help of medium Leanne Rosko

Doty to share in a higher perspective and channel any messages Tamarin may have for us.

Leanne did not disappoint. Immediately she communicated, "Tamarin just said to me, 'it's like, I am not gone. I am here beside you.'"

Leanne continued, "To her there is no separation, and she does admit that she forgets that because she is not in a body. And I don't even know if she needs to come back into a body unless she chooses to in the future. I don't think she needs to come back."

Leanne then asked Tamarin, "Are you excited for what the Earth changes are? Are you hopeful for humanity?"

Leanne reiterated what she heard Tam say. "She is hopeful for humanity," Leanne explained. "She is holding space for humanity and helping others get through it or helping others 'cross through the veil,' Tamarin just said."

"Wow," Leanne shouted. "She just hit me with energy, I've got goose bumps!"

Then, Leanne continued, "Yes, Tamarin is helping others transition from this life. She is holding open the veil for them. And she prefers, she is saying, to hold open the veil when they are still in their bodies so they can see the wonderment of it. To not feel like they must leave their bodies to remember. She really wants to hold open the wonderment for them."

I then quickly chimed in, "Yes, interesting, because Tam was sick for so long, she went in and out of her body a lot—in the car, at dialysis, even in restaurants."

Leanne continued, "Tamarin feels that when we are healthy and more robust, we have a certain resistance to the other side, but with her because she was in and out of her body, she was connected and there was no denying that connection."

"We are all connected," Leanne said. "But Tamarin couldn't deny the connection because of how her body was not the boundary anymore. Her body couldn't be the star of the show, even though it was the star of the show. She had to find a new way to be here and that was her grace in being."

"Wow," I responded and then asked, "Does Tamarin have a message for us?"

"Yes, let's see," Leanne replied, and then she channeled Tam:

There is no coincidence that all of this is coming together in the way that we had planned. And I say we had planned because this has been planned since before I even arrived. And, yes, of course, it is coming to fruition after I leave, but there is my involvement in it, all the way around.

You've brought a great skill into this lifetime, this great skill of communicating, even if you don't even say anything. You hold space for others to feel safe. And that is what this is about now. It is about others feeling safe to enter into awareness, enter into an energy of something that many are uncertain of and afraid to look at, let alone face—that the absolute truth about living is dying.

There has been so much fear on this planet about death, but it is a beautiful experience. It is a wonderful graduation, and yet so many in the physical form run from it and try to evade it.

So, I will say that there is no reason to run from this door, for it is coming to us all eventually. But we can join with it as opposed to running away from it.

In saying this to others, you have then rolled out the carpet so to speak for them to sit and be in peace with what is and to not be resistant, for it's going to come to us all.

I knew it, and yes, I wanted to run the other way, but I couldn't even get up, could I? So, I had to sit, and I had to face it and that is what was so glorious; that I was able to really come into a sense of agreement with it and know that there is a contact there. There is a beautiful energy; a beautiful reality that I was walking into.

And I know you will come to me one day. Do I want you to come today? No thank you. But I know you will come. And so, I would say that is what you are bringing with all of this. You are bringing together an instrument for others to play and get attuned to its music, so they'll not have as much fear about how life will progress. Then, when death comes to call, they will run into it. They will join it and love it and not feel afraid of it. And that is what I wish my message to be.

"Wow! That is beautiful," we both responded in unison when Tam was done.

What a wonderful blessing it is to embrace death of the physical body with open arms. How glorious it will be when you enter the Soul state and look back with deepest gratitude for the gifts that were hidden like beautiful pearls in all your Earthly adventures, and for the amount of self-discovery and enlightenment you accomplished within a single lifetime.

That is the power of victory!

And the best news of all is that you don't follow your path to victory alone. The Beings of Light, your teachers and guides, and even your loved ones in spirit are with you guiding, nurturing, and protecting you—every step of the way until you, too, return home to the realms where they reside.

May blessing be with you on your journey.

ACKNOWLEDGEMENTS

Once again, I would like to honor the Beings of Light who guide and protect us on our path through life. Thank you!

I'm especially grateful to my dad, Bo, whose box of wise sayings taught me at a young age to open my mind and think beyond; my mom, Vevie, whose jest for life and love of all people motivates me every day; my other mother, Jeannie, for being a wonderful shoulder to lean on; my sister, Debby, for companionship through thick and thin. I am so grateful for you; my bonus family, Rob, Nik, and Kelli/Geo for your love, laughter, and support all these wonderful years; and, my daughter, Tamarin, whose after-death presence as hawks, rainbows, face/words in the clouds, and names on license plates confirms that, yes indeed, the Soul is eternal.

I would like to acknowledge all NeuroFit® clients, past and present, who've experienced the benefits of Soulercise® first-hand in the NeuroFit Soul Fitness program. Your dedication to self-discovery and enlightenment through NeuroFitness is bringing greater peace and contentment into the world, one Soul at a time.

I would also like to thank the Harrison Group for helping to spread this message. I am especially grateful to Steve Harrison for your wonderful "mission to help you achieve your mission." Because of the services, coaches, and programs you all provide, I am accomplishing my goal one book at a time. And to Jack Canfield, thank you for your remarkable insight and vision for which I am truly grateful.

And finally, deep gratitude to my editor, Doug Childers, whose pruning and polishing once again helped me illuminate the world of Soul consciousness for my readers; and to *the*BookDesigners for another cover that truly "incarnates" my spiritual vision.

Thank you all!

About the Author

CINDY REYNOLDS is the founder of NeuroFit®, a center to "Cross-Train Your Brain" in Mill Valley, California. For the last 12 years, Cindy has built a Brain Fitness program that uses qEEG (quantitative Electroencephalography) Brain Mapping technology to identify the source of presenting symptoms and then applies cutting-edge NeuroTechnology to train your brain.

Inspired by personal tragedies from a young age, Cindy turned within on a journey that led to the discovery of our eternal self within—our Soul. Cindy details these extraordinary events, from which Soulercise and the 7 Steps were born, in her memoir *Soul Seeker: A Journey to Discover—Who am I &What is My Higher Purpose? Soul Seeker* is also available on Amazon.

Cindy is available for speaking engagements and media/podcast interviews. To learn more about upcoming books, online programs, or to contact Cindy visit www.CindyReynolds.com.

www.ingramcontent.com/pod-product-compliance
Lightning Source LLC
Chambersburg PA
CBHW050231120526
44590CB00016B/2044

www.ingramcontent.com/pod-product-compliance
Lightning Source LLC
Chambersburg PA
CBHW050231120526
44590CB00016B/2044